Arthur Schopenhauer, his Life and Philosophy

By Helen Zimmern

Preface

NEARLY a quarter of a century has elapsed since the name of **ARTHUR SCHOPENHAUER** was first pronounced in England.[1] This country may claim to have given the signal for the recognition of a thinker not at the time widely known or eminently honoured in his native land; and although the subsequent expansion of his fame and influence has been principally conspicuous in Germany, indications have not been wanting of a steady growth of curiosity and interest respecting him here. Allusions to him in English periodical literature have of late been frequent, assuming an acquaintance with his philosophy on the reader's part which the latter, it may be feared, does not often possess. The time thus seems to have arrived for such an account of the man and the author as may effect for the general reader what M. Ribot's able French *précis* has already accomplished for the student of mental science, and may prepare the way for the translation of Schopenhauer's capital treatise, understood to be contemplated by an accomplished German scholar now resident among us.

The little volume which owes its existence to these considerations can advance no lofty pretensions either from the biographical or the critical point of view. No new biographical material of importance can be offered now, and there is every reason to believe that none such exists. We must accordingly depend in the main upon the concise memoir by Gwinner—a model of condensation, good taste, and graphic power—supplemented by the heterogeneous and injudicious, yet in many respects invaluable, mass of detail put forth by the philosopher's immediate disciples, Lindner and Frauenstädt. Relying on these sources of information, we have endeavoured to portray for English readers one of the most original and picturesque intellectual figures of our time; with obvious analogies to Johnson, Rousseau, and Byron, nor yielding in interest to any of them, yet a man of unique mould; a cosmopolitan, moreover, exempt from local and national trammels whose mind was formed to be the common possession of his race. The portrait—should the execution have in any degree corresponded with the intention—will, we are convinced, be valued by all who prefer sterling humanity to affectation, who know how to esteem a genuine man. By many it will be deemed unattractive, by some perhaps even forbidding. We shall not be discouraged by cavils grounded upon the fallacy of estimating every man by a uniform conventional standard, without reference to the special mission appointed him in the world. *Il faut que chacun ait les défauts de ses qualités.* Wordsworth's imperturbable egotism, for example, is even more offensive, because less frankly human, than the boisterous arrogance of Schopenhauer. No one, nevertheless, makes this a crime in Wordsworth, it being universally recognised that he needed all his self-complacency to withstand public contumely; that to wish him other than he was would be to wish that England had never possessed a Wordsworth. Schopenhauer needed even more the steeling armour of self-esteem and scorn, inasmuch as the neglect which exasperated him was more general and more protracted, and arose not, as in Wordsworth's case, from the obtuseness of critics, but from the conspiracy of a coterie. The neglected poet or artist, moreover, has the resource of production; resentment begets new effort, affording an outlet for the pent-up wrath which might otherwise have taken shape as a scandal or a crime, but which now appears transfigured into forms of beauty. The capital labour of Schopenhauer's life, on the other hand, admitted of no repetition; and when it seemed to be dishonoured, the author could but sit brooding over his mortification with a bitterness which, after all, never perverted his intellectual conscience, disgusted him with the seemingly unprofitable pursuit of truth, or impaired his loyalty to the few whom he recognised as worthy of his reverence.

It may still be asked whether Schopenhauer's life-work will really bear comparison with his who brought English poetry back to Nature? If publishing a translation of his writings, we should simply refer the inquirer to the works themselves; but we are painfully aware that no such reference can be confidently made to an abstract whose manifold imperfections are only to be palliated by a necessity and an impossibility the necessity for popular treatment in a volume designed for general readers, the impossibility of exhibiting within our limits the multitudinous aspects of what Schopenhauer himself calls his hundred-gated system. Aware of these inevitable shortcomings, we have striven to let him speak as far as possible for himself—with the result, we trust, of establishing for him an incontestable claim to two immense services, wholly independent of the judgment which may be passed upon the peculiarities of his doctrine. By his lucid and attractive treatment he has made speculative philosophy acceptable to the man of culture and accessible to the mass; by his passion for the concrete, and aptitude for dealing with things as well as thoughts, he has set the pregnant example of testing speculation by science. He will captivate one order of minds by his clear decisive tone as one having authority; another by his profound affinity to the devoutest schools of mysticism, startling as this must appear to those unable to conceive of religion unassociated with some positive creed. Perhaps, however, his most interesting aspect is his character as a representative of the Indian intellect—a European Buddhist. The study of Indian wisdom, conducting by another path to conclusions entirely in harmony with the results of natural science, is destined to affect, and is affecting, the European mind in a degree not inferior to the modification accomplished by the renaissance of Hellenic philosophy; but the process is retarded by the national peculiarities of the Indian sages, and the difficulty of naturalising them in Europe. It is, therefore, much to possess a writer like Arthur Schopenhauer, capable of imparting Western form to Eastern ideas, or rather to ideas once solely Eastern; but which, like seeds wafted by the winds, have wandered far from their birthplace to germinate anew in the brain of Europe. Schopenhauer will for ever stand prominent among those who have helped forward the conception of the Universe as Unity, and even if the peculiar form in which he embodied it fails to obtain currency as the most convenient and correct, it will none the less surely rank among the most impressive and sublime.

CHAPTER I - HIS EARLY YEARS

IN the cemetery of Frankfort-on-the-Main, is a gravestone of black Belgian granite, half hidden by evergreen shrubs. It bears the inscription : 'Arthur Schopenhauer:' no more; neither date nor epitaph. The great man who lies buried here had himself ordained this. He desired no fulsome inscriptions on his tomb : he wished to be recorded in his works, and when his friend Dr. Gwinner once asked where he desired to be buried, he replied, 'No matter where; posterity will find me.'

And posterity is beginning to find him at last, though it has taken it a long while; and into no civilised country has this great man's fame penetrated later than to England. True, his name and philosophy are not unknown to a select few ; as witness the able article published as long ago as 1853 in the 'Westminster Review,' when the recluse of whom it treated was still living. This essay was the first and is still by far the most adequate notice of the modern Buddhist that has appeared in this country. To this day, Arthur Schopenhauer's name conveys no distinct impression even to educated readers. It is mostly pronounced in disparagement of his philosophy, and dismissed with the contemptuous epithet, 'Nihilist,' by persons who have never read a line of his writings, or given his mode of thought an hour's consideration.

They know possibly that he was a great pessimist, that "'tis better not to be" may be deemed the key-note of his speculations. They leave out of all regard that these tenets, be they congenial to them or no, are based on a great mind's life-thoughts and correspond in essentials with those held by 300 millions of the human race.

Yet notwithstanding all this, after long years of neglect and contempt, he is forcing the world to consider him. Speculations that continue to increase in respect and influence cannot be dismissed with a sneer. Even David Strauss, the optimist *par excellence*, pays Schopenhauer a grateful tribute in his last work, 'The New Faith and the Old.' As a rule, he remarks, optimism takes things too easily, and for this reason Schopenhauer's references to the colossal part sorrow and evil play in the world are quite in their right place as a counterbalance, though 'every true philosophy is necessarily optimistic, as otherwise she hews down the branch on which she herself is sitting.' An apter and terser illustration is hardly needed to stigmatise such aberrations of thought. Aberrations, however, of such mighty influence and so needful to the complete development of all phases of humanity, that it is imperative upon all who study the history of their own time to know something of this philosopher's mode of thought. The more so as his influence on politics, literature, sociology and art can no longer be contested. Most modern musicians are great admirers of Schopenhauer, especially the followers of Wagner ; some of whom go so far as to say that in order truly to understand the 'music of the future,' it is needful to have begun with his philosophy.

The history of this man, to whom recognition came so late, is not remarkably eventful. It is little else than the record of his thoughts and his works. He had nevertheless seen more of practical life than many a thinker who evolves a system out of his internal consciousness, shut up within the four walls of his study, ignorant of mankind, their needs, and the adaptability of his speculations for their use. Not unjustly does the 'Revue Contemporaine' say of Schopenhauer, *Ce n'est pas un philosophe comme les autres, c'est un philosophe qui a vu le monde.*

Arthur Schopenhauer was born at Danzig, on the 22nd of February, 1788. His family were of Dutch extraction, but had long settled in this ancient Reichstadt, which at his birth still maintained its Hanseatic privileges. Schopenhauer attached great importance to hereditary characteristics, regarding them among the prime factors of life. Without touching upon this contested principle, it would not be just to leave his genealogy disregarded in his biography, more especially as he was in a measure a living illustration of his theory. The Schopenhauers, so far back as we can trace them, appear to have been men of powerful character. In the days of Arthur's great-grandfather Andreas, they were already rich and influential citizens, so that when Peter the Great and the Empress Catherine visited Danzig, his house was selected to lodge the Imperial guests. The story of this visit has been preserved in the memoirs of Johanna Schopenhauer, the philosopher's mother, and is characteristic of the ancestor's prompt resolution and practical good sense. She gives it as told by a centenarian family retainer, who lived to dandle the infant Arthur in his arms.

When the Czar and his consort were shown the house, they went all over it to choose their bedroom. Their choice fell upon a room in which there was neither stove nor fireplace. It was winter, and the difficulty how to heat the room arose, for the cold was bitter. Everyone was at their wits' end, till old Herr Schopenhauer came to their aid. He ordered several barrels of fine brandy to be brought from the cellar; these he emptied over the tiled floor, closed up the room carefully, and set the spirit ablaze. The Czar looked with delight at the flaming mass seething around his feet. Meanwhile precautions were taken to hinder the fire from spreading. When all was burnt out, the Imperial pair laid themselves to rest in the hot steamy air, and awoke next morning feeling neither headache nor discomfort, ready to extol their host and his hospitality in terms as glowing as his brandy.

Andreas' son, Johann Friedrich, greatly enlarged the business, and added to the wealth and importance of the family. In later years he retired, and ended his days in a stately mansion near Danzig, which, until its demolition, bore the Schopenhauer name. His wife was also sprung from a good lineage. With advancing age she grew imbecile ; she had borne her husband an idiotic son, and perhaps contributed the hypochondriacal element so traceable in the powerful-minded grandson and in his father, her youngest son, Heinrich Floris. He was born in 1747, and was early sent out into the world to gain knowledge and practical experience. For many years he lived in France and England. In France he served as clerk in the firm of Bethmann, merchants of Bordeaux. The admirable chief of that house won his whole respect. So greatly was he impressed by his conduct in business and family affairs, that in after years, when desirous to emphasise a command, he would add as final argument: 'Monsieur Bethmann acted thus.' He read the French authors of his century with intelligent interest, and above all he was partial to Voltaire. In the working of the English constitution he took a lively interest, and was so pleased with family life in this country that he seriously contemplated making it his home. This love for England and English ways found expression in his country seat at Oliva, near Danzig, which he furnished after the

English manner and with English comforts. His garden, too, was laid out in the English style. He daily read an English and French newspaper, and encouraged his son from early boyhood to read the 'Times,' from which, he remarked, 'one could learn everything.' These literary tendencies were undoubtedly inherited by Arthur, who preferred foreign philosophers to those of his country, and was never weary of contrasting Voltaire, Helvetius, Locke, and Hume,
with Leibnitz, Fichte, Schelling, and Hegel, commending the former as the only worthy precursors of Kant. He, too, up to his death daily read the 'Times.' Until the German papers began to occupy themselves about him, he rarely condescended to occupy himself with them, a peculiarity less to be condemned on account of their actual inferiority until a comparatively recent period.

Notwithstanding his love for England, Heinrich Schopenhauer returned to his native city, where he entered the business and inherited the bulk of the family property. By this time his character was fully formed. His rectitude, candour, and uncompromising love of truth were remarkable, and won the esteem of his fellow citizens. Fierce, even passionate in his views and prejudices, he did not withal lack the balance and deliberation usually possessed by less excitable natures. The oppressions and iniquities perpetrated by the Prussians against his native city aroused the full vigour of his hate. At the same time he never withheld from the Great Frederick his just meed of praise. Early in life he might indeed, had he wished, have taken office under this monarch. For on his return from his travels he happened to be among the spectators of a review held at Potsdam. The Great Frederick had an eagle eye, and always marked an unusual appearance in a crowd. The elegance of Schopenhauer's dress, his foreign carriage and independent air, attracted the sovereign's notice. The following day he summoned the young man to his cabinet; the interview lasted two hours, during which the King begged, almost commanded him to settle in Prussia. He held out every inducement, promised to exert every influence on his behalf. But it was in vain. The stern republican would not accept patronage from the oppressor of his native city. He never swerved from the family device : *Point de bonheur sans liberté*; and Frederick was reluctantly obliged to let him depart. He could not forget him : by a cabinet order he assured to Heinrich Floris Schopenhauer and his descendants important privileges, of which, however, they appear never to have availed themselves. This trait alone would serve to prove that Arthur Schopenhauer's father was no ordinary man. Another recorded incident confirms this impression.

After the second partition of Poland the Hanseatic republic of Danzig was destined by Frederick the Great to become his prey. In order to cut off supplies from the landside, the place was blockaded by Prussian troops. The general in command was quartered with Johann Schopenhauer, then living in retirement at his country seat. He showed such generous hospitality to his unwelcome guests that the general desired in some manner to evince his gratitude. He had heard that the old man's son, Heinrich, who lived within the walls, owned horses to which he was so attached that his fondness for them had become proverbial. Forage was growing scarce, and the general offered to allow food for Heinrich's horses to enter. This roused the stern patrician's ire. Why should he be distinguished from among his countrymen? Why should he be deemed willing to receive favours from the hated Prussians? He wrote in reply that he thanked the general for his goodwill; his stables were as yet amply provided, and when the stock was exhausted he should cause his horses to be killed.

It might be supposed that a man who so little conformed to conventionalities, and opposed inflexible prejudice to palpable advantage, would scarcely make a good man of business, above all, a good merchant, perhaps next to a lawyer's, the most trimming and time-serving pursuit. Yet the contrary was the case. Heinrich Schopenhauer conducted his business in a manner that won him all respect and admiration. It was not until he was eight and thirty that he contemplated marriage. His choice fell upon Johanna Henriette Trosiener, a pretty girl of eighteen, whose father was member of the Danzig Senate, and though not wealthy, was counted among the city's patricians. He too had travelled and acquired, like his son-in-law, the cosmopolitan culture uncommon in those days. Cheerful and lively by temperament, these qualities were occasionally overshadowed by unrestrained outbursts of passion so violent that people shunned association with him for very fear. According to the testimony of his daughter, these irruptions of senseless fury seized him quite suddenly, often for the most trivial cause. Fortunately his anger was allayed as rapidly as it arose, but while the attack was upon him even the cat and dog would run away in terror. His wife only could mollify him somewhat.

'It needs but a few strokes to recall the picture of my dear gentle mother, Elizabeth, *née Lehmann*,' says Johanna Schopenhauer ; 'she had a small dainty figure, with the prettiest hands and feet, a pair of large very light blue eyes, a very white fine skin, and long silky light brown hair. So much for her outward appearance. Her physique was not adapted to make her the robust housekeeper at that time in fashion; with regard to what is demanded nowadays of women, her education had been no less neglected than that of her contemporaries. She could play a
few polonaises and mazurkas, accompany herself to a few songs, and read and write sufficiently well for household requirements: that was pretty well all she had been taught. But common sense, natural ability, and the quick power of conception common to women, indemnified her for these deficiencies.'

Such were the parents of the young girl, who on the verge of womanhood was united to a man twenty years her senior. Of her youth we have records from her own pen, as she intended writing her Memoirs, which would have proved interesting, not only with regard to her son, but because she lived on terms of friendly intimacy with the famous men and women of her day. Unfortunately she was only able to bring them down to the year 1789, and as she was born in 1766, they embrace the least generally interesting period of her life. They present, however, a good idea of society in those troublous times. Johanna was the eldest daughter of her parents; she inherited her mother's dainty proportions, light brown hair and clear blue eyes. In youth her figure was unusually attractive and *mignonne* ; later in life she became corpulent, which, together with a malformation of the hip, detracted from the charm of her exterior. Her countenance was pleasant, but not beautiful ; till her death she preserved a certain grace in carriage and conversation which everywhere attracted attention. She was very popular, and was fond of social gatherings. Some people thought her haughty, which she was not, but she maintained a certain reserve in her demeanour towards strangers, and was besides fully aware of all her advantages, mental and physical.

This is an account of her marriage in her own words. 'Before I had completed my nineteenth year, a brilliant future was opened out to me by this marriage, more brilliant than I was justified in anticipating, but that these considerations had no weight in my youthful mind upon my final decision will be readily believed. I thought I had done with life, a delusion to which one so easily and willingly gives way in early youth upon the first painful experience. I knew I had cause to be proud of belonging to this man, and I was proud. At the same time I as little feigned ardent love for him, as he demanded it from me.'

Her education had been as incomplete as her mother's, but constant communion with a man of Heinrich Schopenhauer's calibre, united to good natural ability, soon developed her intellectual growth. His house, alone, was an education. It was elegantly furnished so as to foster her sense of refinement; the walls were hung with engravings after the old masters, busts and excellent casts of antique statues ornamented the rooms ; the library was stocked with the best French, German, and English authors. An English clergyman attached to the colony at Danzig, Dr. Jameson, had been her friend and tutor from childhood. Under his guidance she read with judicious care and understanding, so that thanks to his aid and that of her husband, combined with the fruitful soil she herself offered for these endeavours, her mental development was rapid.

The honeymoon of this pair was spent at their country seat of Oliva. They had hardly been married before Heinrich was seized with one of his eager longings to travel. The young wife shared his passion, and they set out upon a long journey. Berlin and Hanover were first visited ; from thence they went to Pyrmont, even then a popular watering place. Here they became acquainted with the statesman Justus Möser, not unjustly entitled the Franklin of Germany. After this they proceeded to Frankfort, with which Johanna was especially delighted, little dreaming that it would become the home of her unborn son, whose name was destined to add another glory to that ancient city.

'I felt as if a draught of native air greeted me in Frankfort,' she says. ' Everything recalled Danzig to me with its busy independent life.'

Belgium was next traversed, then the pair visited Paris, and finally crossed to England. It was the father's wish that his son—for he had determined on the sex—should be born in England, in order that he might enjoy all the rights of English citizenship; and with great reluctance he relinquished his purpose, necessitated by his wife's precarious state of health. The journey fell in the depth of winter, and was attended with hardships of which the present generation can form no idea. It was, however, safely accomplished. On the 22nd of February, 1788, the great pessimist first saw the light of a world he deemed so wretched. The house in which he was born still stands, though greatly altered. It is No. 117, Heiligengeiststrasse, in Danzig.

An anecdote of his birthday has been preserved. His father, it appears, was distinguished by intellectual, rather than personal attractions. He was short and clumsily made, his broad face was lighted by prominent eyes, only redeemed from ugliness by their intelligence, his nose was stumpy and upturned, his mouth large and wide. From early youth too he had been deaf. When, on the afternoon of the 22nd of February, he entered his counting-house, and laconically announced to the assembled clerks : 'A son,' the merry book-keeper, relying upon his principal's deafness, exclaimed, to the general amusement : 'If he is like his papa he will be a pretty baboon.' His prophecy was tolerably fulfilled; excepting that Arthur boasted a splendid forehead and penetrating light blue eyes, he resembled his father in build of face and figure.

The child was baptised on the third of March, in the Marienkirche, one of the finest old churches of the Baltic regions. He was called Arthur, because the name remains the same in all European languages, a circumstance regarded as advantageous to a merchant; for to that career the nine-days'-old child was already destined by his circumspect father.

Of the first few years of his life we know nothing. His infancy was contemporaneous with the French Revolution, a political event in which his parents took the liveliest interest, and which naturally aroused all his father's keen republicanism. In 1793 occurred the blockade of Danzig; it was then the incident regarding the horses took place. Heinrich Schopenhauer was firmly resolved to forsake his native city in case of its subjugation by the Prussians ; never would he consent to live under their detested rule. He would rather sacrifice home and fortune. When Danzig's fate was decided, in March, 1793, he did not hesitate one moment to put his resolve into execution. Within twenty-four hours of the entry of the Prussian troops, when he saw that all hope was lost, he, his wife, and little five-year-old son, fled to Swedish Pomerania. Thence they made their way to Hamburg, a sister Hanseatic town, which retained its old freedom and privileges, and was therefore a congenial home for the voluntary exiles. This uncompromising patriotism cost Heinrich Schopenhauer more than a tenth of his fortune, so highly was he taxed for leaving. But he heeded nothing save his rectitude and his principles, qualities his son inherited. His fearless love of truth and honest utterance of his opinion were as marked as his father's.

Schopenhauer family house in Hamburg.

The family now established their domicile in Hamburg. They were kindly received by the best families, and a new pleasant life opened in place of that left behind. Whether because too old to be transplanted, or from other causes, Heinrich Schopenhauer had not long removed to Hamburg ere he was seized with an almost morbid desire to travel. His wife's joyous temperament, her *savoir faire*, her perfect mastery of foreign languages, and the ease with which she formed new acquaintances, made her a desirable travelling companion. During the twelve years of their residence at Hamburg many longer and shorter journeys were undertaken, besides which Johanna visited her own people every four years. To Danzig her husband did not accompany her ; he never would re-enter the city. Thus the restlessness engendered by her ill-assorted union found vent in excitement and recreation.

Arthur always accompanied his parents. The education he thus gained was an additional inducement for these trips, and one his father held as by no means least important. Above all, he was anxious his son should have cosmopolitan training, see everything, judge with his own eyes, and be free from those prejudices that too fatally doom 'home-keeping youths' to 'homely wits.' Arthur ever expressed himself thankful for this inestimable advantage ; it exercised great influence upon his life, his character, and his philosophy. True, this nomad existence interfered with the even course of a school education, and hindered the systematic acquirement of ordinary branches of knowledge ; but this was in great measure compensated by the open intelligence it fostered, and entirely redeemed when the youth applied himself strenuously to repair these shortcomings. On the other hand, travel brought him into contact at an early age with some of the best minds of the time. As a child he was acquainted with many celebrities, such as **Baroness Staël**, Klopstock, Keimarus, Madame Chevalier, Nelson, and **Lady Hamilton**.

Once, about his nineteenth year, when he found himself deficient in general information in comparison with other youths, he was inclined to regret his abnormal boyhood. The feeling passed never to return. His clear intelligence recognised that the course his life had taken had not been the consequence of chance, but needful to his complete development. For in early youth, when the mind is most prone to receive impressions, and stretches its feelers in all directions, he was made acquainted with actual facts and realities, instead of living in a world of dead letters and bygone tales, like most youths who receive an academic education. To this he attributed much of the freshness and originality of his style : he had learnt, in practical intercourse with men and the world, not to rest satisfied with the mere sound of words, or to take them for the thing itself.

In Arthur's ninth year, his parents undertook a journey through France. On its conclusion they left the boy behind them at **Havre** with a M. Gregoire, a business friend. Here he remained two years, and was educated together with M. Gregoire's son. His father's object was that Arthur should thoroughly master the French language, an object so completely realized that when he came back to Hamburg it was found he had forgotten his native tongue, and was forced to learn it again like a foreigner. Arthur frequently recalled these two years spent in France as the happiest of his boyhood.

When he had once more accustomed himself to the sound of German, he was sent to school. Here his instruction was entirely conducted with a view to the requirements of the future merchant, and the classics were therefore almost, if not wholly, disregarded. It was soon after that he evinced a decided bent towards the study of philosophy. He entreated his father to grant him the happiness of a collegiate education, a request that met with stern refusal. Heinrich Floris had determined that his son should be a merchant, and old Schopenhauer was not accustomed to be baulked. As time went on, and he saw this yearning was no passing fancy, he condescended to give it more serious consideration, especially as the testimony of the masters endorsed Arthur's prayers. He almost yielded; but the thought of the poverty too often attendant on a votary of the muses, was so repugnant to the life-plans he had formed for his only son, that he determined on a last resort to divert the boy from his purpose. He took refuge in stratagem to effect what he was too just to accomplish by force. He brought the lad's desires into conflict by playing off his love of travelling, and his eagerness to visit his dear friend young Gregoire, against his longing to study philosophy. He put this alternative : either to enter a high school, or to accompany his parents upon a journey of some years' duration, planned to embrace France, England, and Switzerland. If he chose the latter, he was to renounce all thought of an academical career, and to enter business on returning to Hamburg.

It was a hard condition to impose on a boy of fifteen, but the plot had been well laid. The lad could not withstand the inducement; he decided in favour of travel, and turned his back upon learning, as he deemed, for ever.

Of this journey Johanna Schopenhauer wrote a lively account, culling her materials from the copious diary she kept. Her son, too, was encouraged to keep a journal, in order to stimulate accurate observation. The tour included Belgium, France, Switzerland, Germany, and England, and lasted over two years. While his parents made a trip to the north of Britain, Arthur was left at a school in Wimbledon. It was kept by a clergyman, and the boy appears to have been greatly plagued by his master's orthodox theology. It was then doubtless that he laid the foundation for the fierce hatred of English bigotry, derided in his works. Here too he gained his accurate knowledge of the language and literature, with which his school-time was chiefly occupied. His recreations were gymnastics and flute playing.

When the family visited Switzerland, Arthur was overwhelmed with the majesty of the Alps. He could not satiate his gaze with their beauty, and when his parents desired to go further, he entreated to be left at Chamounix, that he might still longer enjoy this glorious sight. Mont Blanc, above all, was the Alp to which he gave his whole heart ; and those who knew him in later life say that he never, even then, could speak of that mountain without a certain tone of sadness and yearning. He touches on this in 'Die Welt als Wille und Vorstellung':

'The sad disposition so often remarked in highly gifted men, has its emblem in this mountain with its cloud-capped summit. But when at time, perchance at dawn, the veil of mist is torn asunder, and the peak, glowing with the sun's reflection, looks down on Chamounix from its celestial height above the clouds, it is a spectacle which stirs every soul to its inmost depths. Thus the most melancholy genius will at times show signs of a peculiar cheerfulness of disposition, which springs from the complete objectiveness of his intellect, and is possible only to him. It hovers like a halo about his noble forehead : *in tristitia hilaris, in hilaritate tristis*.'

In the autumn of this year (1804) Arthur went to Danzig to receive confirmation in the same venerable Marienkirche that had witnessed his baptism. With the new year he entered a merchant's office, true to his promise. It was hateful to him, but he tried to resign himself. He honoured and respected his father, and held his wish to be law.

A very few months after he had the misfortune to lose this parent, who fell from an attic window into the canal. It had always been his custom to inspect everything in person, and that would sufficiently account for his presence in this part of his warehouse. Report, however, spread that Heinrich Schopenhauer had committed suicide on account of fancied pecuniary loss. He had in truth suffered lately from attacks of over- anxiety, which were thus interpreted as signs of mental derangement. His increased deafness may have helped to foster his violent attacks of passionate anger, which certainly broke out more frequently during the last months of his life. These circumstances combined lent an air of credibility to a rumour often used in after years as a cruel weapon against his son.

Arthur never ceased to reverence his father's memory. An instance of this respect is observable in his remark regarding the mercantile profession. 'Merchants are the only honest class of men : they avow openly that money-making is their object, while others pursue the same end, hiding it hypocritically under cover of an ideal vocation.'

The collected edition of his works was intended to be prefaced by a splendid memorial of his filial gratitude. For some cause this preface was omitted. It deserves quotation as throwing an agreeable light upon a man whom we shall not always find so lovable.

'Noble, beneficent spirit! to whom I owe all that I am, your protecting care has sheltered and guided me not only through helpless childhood and thoughtless youth, but in manhood and up to the present day. When bringing a son such as I am into the world, you made it possible for him to exist and to develop his individuality in a world like this. Without your protection, I should have perished an hundred times over. A decided bias, which made only one occupation congenial, was too deeply rooted in my very being for me to do violence to my nature, and force myself, careless of existence, at best to devote my intellect merely to the preservation of my person ; my sole aim in life how to procure my daily bread. You seem to have understood this ; to have known beforehand that I should hardly be qualified to till the ground, or to win my livelihood by devoting my energies to any mechanical craft. You must have foreseen that your son, oh proud republican! would not endure to crouch before ministers and councillors, Maecenases and their satellites, in company with mediocrity and servility, in order to beg ignobly for bitterly earned bread; that he could not bring himself to flatter puffed-up insignificance, or join the sycophantic throng of charlatans and bunglers ; but that, as your son, he would think, with the Voltaire whom you honoured, "*Nous n'avons que deux jours a vivre : il ne vaut pas la peine de les passer a ramper devant les joquins meprisables.*"

'Therefore I dedicate my work to you, and call after you to your grave the thanks I owe to you and to none other. "*Nam Caesar nullus nobis haec otia fecit.*"

'That I was able to cultivate the powers with which nature endowed me, and put them to their proper use ; that I was able to follow my innate bias, and think and work for many, while none did aught for me : this I owe to you, my father, I owe it to your activity, your wisdom, your frugality, your forethought for the future. Therefore I honour you, my noble father ; and therefore, whosoever finds any pleasure, comfort, or instruction in my work, shall learn your name, and know that if Heinrich Floris Schopenhauer had not been the man he was, Arthur Schopenhauer would have stumbled an hundred times. Let my gratitude render the only homage possible towards you, who have ended life : let it bear your name as far as mine is capable of carrying it.'

CHAPTER II - HIS STUDENT YEARS

THUS at seventeen, Arthur Schopenhauer was thrown on his own resources, for the chasm that divided him from his mother made itself felt immediately upon the father's death. The want of harmony among the strangely assorted elements of this family is scarcely astonishing. This circumstance, recognised or dimly discerned, probably explains their restlessness and preference for a nomadic existence. The abyss had not yet opened between mother and son, but the mental estrangement that must have existed for years evinced itself as soon as they were brought into personal contact, which up to this time had been little the case. Johanna Schopenhauer's volatility, optimism, and love of pleasure, repelled her son, and ever remained a puzzle to him, who, philosopher though he was, failed to make sufficient allowance for peculiarity of temperament, and condemned unsparingly whatever crossed his views. Neither could the mother understand her son, who fostered gloomy ideas of life, loved solitude, and was maddened beyond endurance by the social cackle politely termed conversation.

Arthur felt his father's loss acutely. To show deference to his memory he continued the hated mercantile pursuits, though daily his being rebelled more and more against the monotonous and soulless office routine. To be chained for life, as he thought, to a path so distasteful, deepened his depression.

Meanwhile Frau Schopenhauer made use of her liberty to remove to Weimar, then in the zenith of its glory as a centre of *beaux esprits*. Here her light-hearted spirit hoped to find more congenial ground than among the respectable Hamburg burghers, whose social meetings were all pervaded by a heavy commercial air, abhorrent to her aesthetic soul. Nor was she mistaken. Though the time of her arrival coincided with great historical convulsions,—just a fortnight before the battle of Jena and the military occupation of Weimar, a time therefore little adapted to the formation of social relations,—Frau Schopenhauer's energies and talent for society overcame all obstacles. In an incredibly short space she had formed a *salon*, collecting round her most of the great stars of that brilliant *coterie*.

To quote the words of her daughter, Adele, prefixed to her mother's unfinished memoirs, 'The time which followed (after the father's death), endowed her with a second spring of life, for Heaven granted to her then what is usually the privilege of early youth. With warm untroubled feelings she gazed into a world unrealized till then, though dreamt of long ago. Surprised at the rapid growth of her abilities, exalted by the sudden development of a latent talent, she experienced ever fresh delight in intercourse with the celebrated men resident at Weimar, or attracted thither by its stars. She was liked ; her society was agreeable. Her circumstances still permitted her to live in comfort, and to surround herself almost daily with her rich circle of friends. Her modest, pleasing manners made her house a centre of intellectual activity, where everyone felt at home, and freely contributed the best he had to bring. In the outline of her memoirs she names a few of the interesting men who frequented the salon. Numberless others came and went in the course of years, for despite all outward changes, her house long retained a faint afterglow of those halcyon days.'

Among these names figure European celebrities. First and foremost the mighty Goethe; then the brothers Schlegel and Grimm, Prince Pickler, Fernow (whose biography was Johanna Schopenhauer's literary *début*), Wieland, Meyer, &c. At court, too, the lively widow was a welcome guest. The terrible October days (1806) when Weimar woke to hear the thundering cannons of Jena, made but a temporary interruption to this intellectual life. The pillage of Weimar furnished Johanna Schopenhauer with matter for a lively letter to her son. She interrupted her narrative, however, by saying: 'I could tell you things that would make your hair stand on end, but I refrain, for I know how you love to brood over human misery in any case.'

This remark is characteristic and valuable, as it demonstrates the innateness of Schopenhauer's pessimism, and unanswerably refutes the contention of his adversaries, who choose to see in his philosophic views nothing but the wounded vanity and embittered moroseness of a disappointed man. This view will not apply to the case of a youth, nurtured in the lap of riches, who had led an independent, careless and interesting life. It is true he had lived through a year of bitter days, cooped up in an office, pursuing a detested vocation ; but a year's wretchedness, even though he at the time deemed it permanent, could not have developed in a healthy temperament such a deep disgust of life.

Still not even the reverence he paid his father's memory could keep him steadily to office work. He played truant to attend Gall's phrenological lectures; he wrote out his own thoughts under the cover of ledgers and letters ; he had abandoned all hope of making good his mistaken career, but he could not renounce all intercourse with learning. His melancholy increased, his letters abounded with invectives on his blighted fate. These complaints reached his mother, who for once could sympathise with her son. She consulted her Weimar friends concerning him, and received the comforting assurance that it was not too late for him to retrace his steps ; an assurance she hastened to communicate to Arthur, who received the news with a flood of tears. With impulsive decision he threw up business and hastened to Gotha, where, by the advice of Fernow, he was to enter upon his academic studies. He took private lessons in Greek and Latin, besides the usual curriculum; his progress was so rapid that the professors prophesied for him a brilliant future as a classical scholar, and his German writings showed a maturity of thought and expression that astounded everyone. Schopenhauer laid great stress upon the acquisition of ancient languages, and defended the study of Greek and Latin with all the ardour of a fanatical philologist, weighted with the heavy artillery of abusive utterance that characterised his speech and writing. Heine calls the Nibelungen-Lied an epic written with granite boulders. The criticism would not ill apply to Schopenhauer's massive, bold, lucid and relentless style.

Should the time ever come when the spirit that is bound up with the languages of the ancients shall vanish from our higher education, then barbarity, vulgarity and commonplace, will take possession of all literature. For the works of the ancients are the pole-star of every artistic and literary effort; if that sinks, you are lost. Already the bad, careless style of most modern authors shows that they have never written Latin. Occupation with the writers of antiquity has been aptly termed "humanitarian study," for through them the scholar becomes a man; they usher him into a world free from the exaggerations of the Middle Ages and the Romantic School, which afterwards so deeply permeated European civilization, that even now, everyone enters life imbued with them, and must strip them off before he can be a man. Do not think your modern wisdom can ever prove a substitute for this regeneration; you are not born freemen like the Greeks and Romans; you are not unspoilt children of nature. You are above all the sons and heirs of the barbarous Middle Ages, with their absurdities, their disgraceful priestcraft, their half-brutal, half-ridiculous chivalry. Though both are coming to an end, you are not yet capable of standing alone. Without classical culture, your literature will degenerate into idle talk and dull pedantry. Your authors, guiltless of Latin, will sink to the level of gossiping barbers. I must censure one special abuse, which daily stalks forth more insolently: it is this, that in scientific books and in learned journals issued by academies, quotations from the Greek, and even those from the Latin, are given in a German translation. Fie, for shame! do you write for tailors and cobblers? I almost think you do, to command a large sale. Then permit me most humbly to remark that you are common fellows in every sense of the word. Have more honour in your souls and less money in your pockets, and let the uncultured man feel his inferiority, instead of scraping bows to his money-box. A German translation of Greek and Latin authors is a substitute similar to that which gives chicory in place of coffee; besides which you cannot even depend on its accuracy.'

Schopenhauer's success at Gotha cheered him and gave him renewed interest in life. He threw aside the apathy that had begun to envelope him at Hamburg, and entered heart and soul into his studies. Nor did this confine itself to study : Arthur Schopenhauer, the misanthrope, actually turned man of the world, *pro tem.* : sought the society of aristocrats, dressed with scrupulous care (a habit he retained through life), wore the newest-shaped garments, and squandered so much money that even his easy going mother urged him to practise more economy. His course at Gotha came to a sudden end, after six months' residence. A professor named Schulze, personally unknown to Schopenhauer, had publicly made some uncomplimentary remarks on the German class to which he belonged. Considering that the Professor had been wanting in the respect due to German gymnasiasts, Schopenhauer, with all the ardour of youth, gave vent to some sarcastic speeches on the subject, which, though delivered privately, were reported to the master, whose petty nature could not bear the irritation of sarcasm. He swore revenge, and succeeded in inducing Schopenhauer's private tutor, Doring, to discontinue his instructions. Under these circumstances, Schopenhauer held it to be incompatible with his honour to remain in the Gymnasium; he quitted Gotha in the autumn of 1807 and proceeded to Weimar. There he continued his preparatory collegiate studies. Weimar attracted him; he preferred to remain here rather than follow his mother's wishes, and enter another gymnasium. He did not, however, live under her roof, at her express desire.

'It is needful to my happiness,' she wrote to him shortly before his arrival, 'to know that you are happy, but not to be a witness of it. I have always told you it is difficult to live with you; and the better I get to know you, the more I feel this difficulty increase, at least for me. I will not hide it from you : as long as you are what you are, I would rather bring any sacrifice than consent to live with you. I do not undervalue your good points, and that which repels me does not lie in your heart; it is in your outer, not your inner being; in your ideas, your judgment, your habits; in a word, there is nothing concerning the outer world in which we agree. Your ill-humour, your complaints of things inevitable, your sullen looks, the extraordinary opinions you utter, like oracles none may presume to contradict; all this depresses me and troubles me, without helping you. Your eternal quibbles, your laments over the stupid world and human misery, give me bad nights and unpleasant dreams.'

In consequence of this letter, Schopenhauer settled in lodgings in Weimar. In the same house lived Franz Passow, two years his senior, who had also devoted himself to classical learning at Gotha, under Professor Jacobs, and who subsequently became a distinguished philologist. With Passow's aid and supervision, Scopenhauer penetrated yet further into the mysteries and riches of classical lore. His natural aptitude for learning languages helped him to repair lost time with incredible rapidity. He laboured day and night at Greek, Latin, Mathematics, and History, allowing nothing to divert his attention. Thus passed two rich busy years of mental culture, barren of external events save one : Schopenhauer's visit to Erfurt, where he was present at the famous congress of 1808, where kings and princes were plentiful as blackberries, and Napoleon, then at the acme of his power, lorded it over the assembly. He appears to have gained admission to the theatre, and seen the wonderful sight it presented when Talma and a chosen Parisian troupe played the finest tragedies of France before this 'parterre of kings.' He unsparingly lashes the contemptible frivolity of the court ladies, who cried down with Napoleon, as a 'monster,' before this evening, and after it cried him up again as 'the most amiable man in the world.'

On attaining his twenty-first year, in 1809, Schopenhauer decided on studying at the University of Gottingen, where he matriculated in the medical faculty. His stupendous energy never abated. During the first year of his residence he heard lectures on Constitutional History, Natural History, Mineralogy, Physics, Botany, and the History of the Crusades, besides reading at home on all cognate matters. He then passed into the philosophical faculty, devoting his attention to Plato and Kant, before attempting the study of Aristotle and Spinoza. Combined with his philosophical curriculum, he found time to attend lectures on Astronomy, Meteorology, Physiology, Ethnography, and Jurisprudence. He laid great stress on the advantages of *viva voce* instruction, though he has also admitted, in one of his manuscript books, c that the dead word of a great man is worth incomparably more than the *viva vox* of a blockhead.'

These manuscript books were a peculiarity of Schopenhauer's during all his university career. In them he noted down not only all he heard delivered, but his own criticisms and comments. He is often at variance with his masters, and says so in no measured terms, destroying their vantage ground with his relentless logic, or by some apt quotation. The many-sidedness of his acquirements becomes more and more remarkable as these note-books are perused. This trait is apt to bring superficiality in its train ; not so, however, with Schopenhauer, who applied himself with thoroughness to every subject he took in hand. He prided himself on his knowledge of the physical sciences, and always laid stress upon them when speaking of his philosophic system, largely influenced by this catholicity, for his works abound with illustrations drawn from all branches of science. To this he owed his large-mindedness, his scope; it is this separates him so widely from the generality of philosophers whose arguments and instances are solely derived from psychology. He had seen the world, he had studied the varied branches of human interests ; he was therefore competent to give an opinion. He acknowledges the fact when he says: 'This is why I can speak with authority, and I have done so honourably.' Later he writes on this subject to a disciple:

'I pray you, do not write on physiology in its relation to psychology, without having digested Cabanis and Bichat *in succum et sanguinem* ; in return you may leave a hundred German scribblers unread. At best the study of psychology is vain, for there is no Psyche ; men cannot be studied alone, but in connection with the world Microkosmus and Macrokosmus combined as I have done. And test yourself whether you really possess and comprehend physiology, which presupposes a knowledge of anatomy and chemistry.'

The records of his life, apart from studies, are meagre. He was certainly no German student in that ordinary acceptation of the word which implies a youth addicted to the imbibition of innumerable bumpers of beer, to playing of mad pranks, and duelling on the smallest provocation. Schopenhauer was a sworn enemy to the foolish practice of duelling, and has exposed its absurdities with his biting sarcasm and unerring logic. He treats its intellectual rather than its ethical aspect; disdaining to give emphasis to the palpable paradox that blind heathens had ignored the sublime principles of honour which are held as exigent by the followers of the gentle Preacher of the Mount. He shows how the point of honour does not depend on a man's own words and actions, but on another's, so that the reputation of the noblest and wisest may hinge on the tattling of a fool, whose word, if he chooses to abuse his fellow, is regarded as an unalterable decree, only capable of reversal by blood shedding ; disproof being of no avail. Superior strength, practice, or chance, decides the question in debate. There are various forms of insult; to strike a person is an act of such grave magnitude that it causes the moral death of the person struck; while all other wounded honour can be healed by a greater or lesser amount of blood, this insult needs complete death to afford its cure.

Only those conversant with the absurd lengths to which duelling has been carried at the German universities can fully appreciate Schopenhauer's bitterness. This essay on duelling was not published till the last years of his life, but it is incontestable that the youth shared the sage's views and acted upon them.

The only fellow-students Schopenhauer mentioned especially were Bunsen and an American, who had been attracted to him by his knowledge of English. The two were his habitual dinner companions. Schopenhauer later dwelt on the singular chance that made the three each realise in their person the three possible spheres of happiness he admits; dividing all possessions into what a man is, that which he has, and that which he represents. The American became a noted millionaire ; in Bunsen, Schopenhauer never recognised anything but a diplomatist, he ignored his literary activity, saying that a better Hebrew scholar was required to translate the Scriptures, and as for 'God in History,' that was only another name for Bunsen in History. His own lot he deemed the most important, though not the happiest or the most dazzling—that of a marked individuality. Bunsen, somewhat his senior, was warmly attached to Schopenhauer during their Göttingen residence, and hopes had been held out that he would furnish some biographical matter. But he died too soon after his early friend to admit of their realisation.

Before Schopenhauer quitted Göttingen he was fully assured that his bias was bent towards philosophy. Though ardently impressionable, he never carried enhusiasm beyond calm analytical judgment; and that he clearly recognised the sound core as well as the exterior prickles of the fruit for which he abandoned the active world, is proved by a letter written at this period.

'Philosophy is an alpine road, and the precipitous path which leads to it is strewn with stones and thorns. The higher you climb, the lonelier, the more desolate grows the way; but he who treads it must know no fear; he must leave everything behind him; he will at last have to cut his own path through the ice. His road will often bring him to the edge of a chasm, whence he can look into the green valley beneath. Giddiness will overcome him, and strive to draw him down, but he must resist and hold himself back. In return, the world will soon lie far beneath him ; its deserts and bogs will disappear from view; its irregularities grow indistinguishable; its discords cannot pierce so high; its roundness becomes discernible. The climber stands amid clear fresh air, and can behold the sun when all beneath is still shrouded in the blackness of night.'

Schopenhauer spent his vacations at Weimar, with the exception of one excursion into the Harz Mountains. In 1811 he quitted Göttingen for the University of Berlin, where he once more pursued a varied course of studies with eager energy. That first winter he attended Fichte's lectures on Philosophy, besides classes on Experimental Chemistry, Magnetism and Electricity, Ornithology, Amphibiology, Ichthyology, Domestic Animals, and Norse Poetry. Between the years 1812-13 he heard Schleiermacher read on the ' History of Philosophy since the time of Christ,' Wolf on the 'Clouds' of Aristophanes, the 'Satires' of Horace, and Greek antiquities, still continuing his natural history studies of Physics, Astronomy, General Physiology, Zoology, and Geology. How carefully he followed, his copious note-books prove. The most characteristic are those relating in any way to philosophy. His annotations grow more and more independent; the elements of his own system become more traceable as he differs from his professors, and explains his reasons for diverging from the beaten track. He does not hesitate to controvert their assertions, in language of unmistakable distinctness, occasionally in sarcasms more biting than refined. This habit of employing strong expressions increased with Schopenhauer's years, and is greatly to be regretted, as he could have easily been equally emphatic without recourse to a practice that exposed him to the imputation of vulgarity. This exercise of the clumsy weapons of abuse in place of dignified controversy is a serious blot on the escutcheon of German men of learning, and is doubly regrettable in Schopenhauer, who possessed a facility of wielding his native tongue quite unusual with ordinary writers, who seem to hold that the value of the matter is in inverse proportion to the merit of the manner. Schopenhauer's style was from the first clear, classical, and exact ; a circumstance he attributed in a great degree to his early training, which had been directed towards the more terse and nervous English and French authors in preference to the verbose German. It is this that makes the Germans so pre-eminently unreadable; and one of Schopenhauer's chief claims to hearing is his happy art of adapting himself to the meanest capacity. It is no small merit to say of a philosopher that his works will never stand in need of an expounder.

It was Fichte's fame that drew Schopenhauer to Berlin ; he hoped to find in his lectures the quintessence of philosophy, but his ' reverence *a priori* ' soon gave place to 'contempt and gibes.' The mystical sophistry and insolent mannerism of speech into which Fichte had drifted revolted Schopenhauer, who liked everything to be clear and logical. Fichte's personality repelled him, as well as his delivery. He would often imitate the little red-haired man trying to impose upon his hearers with the hollow pathos of such phrases as : ' The world is, because it is; and is as it is, because it is so.' Notwithstanding this speedy disenchantment, Schopenhauer continued to hear these abstruse discourses, and eagerly disputed their dicta in the hours devoted to controversy. His notes abound in criticisms of Fichte. He heads the manuscript book devoted to this purpose with the words 'Wissenschaftslehre,' and writes in the margin, Perhaps the more correct reading is 'Wissenschaftsleere,' playing on the resemblance of the words study and emptiness; thus, the study of science and the emptiness of science. In another place he complains of the difficulty he finds in following Fichte. His delivery, he says, is clear and deliberate enough, but he dwells so long on things easy to comprehend, repeating the same idea in other words, that the attention flags with listening to that which is already understood, and becomes distracted.

Schopenhauer regarded an expression used in one of the first lectures he heard as so striking a proof of psychological ignorance as almost to unfit its holder to the title of philosopher. Fichte asserted that genius and madness are so little allied that they may be regarded as utterly divergent, defining genius as godlike, madness as bestial. To this lecture Schopenhauer appends a lengthy criticism, which contains the complete germ of his own Theory of Genius:—

'I do not hold that the maniac is like an animal, and that the healthy reason stands midway between insanity and genius ; on the contrary, I believe that genius and insanity, though widely different, are yet more nearly related than is the one to ordinary reason and the other to animality. An intelligent dog may be more properly compared to an average, well balanced, intelligent man, than to a maniac (not an idiot). On the other hand, lives of men of genius show that they are often excited like maniacs before the world. According to Seneca, Aristotle says: "*Nullum magnum ingenium sine insanise mixtura.*" I affirm that a healthy intelligent man is firmly encased by the corporeal conditions of thought and consciousness (such as are furnished by space, time and definite ideas); they enfold him closely, fit and cover him like a well-made dress. He cannot get beyond them (that is, he cannot conceive of himself and of things in the abstract, without those conditions of experience); but within these bounds he is at home. The same thing holds good of a healthy animal, only that its conception of experience is less clear; its dress, we might say, is uncomfortable, and too wide. Genius, in virtue of a transcendental power which cannot be defined, sees through the limitations which are the conditions of a conception of experience, seeks all his life long to communicate this knowledge, and acts by its light.

To continue my simile, we might say that genius is too ample for its dress, and is not wholly clad by it. The conditions of a conception of experience have been disturbed for the maniac ; his laws of experience have been destroyed, for these laws do not pertain to the things themselves, but to the manner in which our senses conceive them (which is confirmed in this case); everything is embroiled for him; according to my simile, his dress is torn, but just for that very reason his ego, which is subject to no disturbance, looks through occasionally. Maniacs make remarks full of genius, or rather would make them, if that clear consciousness which is the very essence of genius were not wanting. . . . Take for instance King Lear, who is certainly correctly drawn ; is he nearer to animality or genius ?

'On the other hand, genius often resembles insanity; because, by dint of looking at things in the abstract, it is less acquainted with the world of experience, and, like the maniac, confuses ideas by realising things in the abstract at the same time. Just as Shakespere's Lear is a representation of insanity combined with genius, so Goethe's Tasso is a representation of genius combined with insanity. The idiot is more like an animal; to continue my simile, I should say that he has shrivelled up, and cannot fill out his dress, which hangs loosely about him; far from looking out beyond it, he cannot even move about in it freely; he is completely like an animal. Every stupid person approaches this condition, more or less. Of every worldly-wise man the contrary is true, his dress fits him like a glove. From animality and idiotcy we arrive by degrees to the greatest cleverness. But genius and insanity are not the first and the last steps of the series, but integrally different, as I have said.'

Schopenhauer's disparaging opinion of Fichte has been quoted as a proof of conceit, but passages in his works prove that it did not spring from mere arrogance. He opposed the common error that Fichte had continued the metaphysical system raised by Kant, and contended that on the contrary he had absolutely swerved from his master's tenets, which were far more those of searching logic than of misty metaphysics. He is fair, too ; a marginal note to one of the propositions in the course of Fichte's lectures on 'Wissenschaftslehre' reads: 'Though this be madness, yet there's method in it.' Occasionally he breaks off his memorandum, saying that owing to the obscure phrases bandied, the air had grown so dark in the lecture room that he could not see to write, and that the lecturer had only provided a tallow candle to illuminate the hall. Or, again, when Fichte repeats the words 'seeing,' 'visibility,' 'pure light,' Schopenhauer writes in the margin : 'As he put up the pure light today instead of the tallow candle, this *précis* could not be continued.' At another time he remarks : ' It was so dark in the hall that Fichte was able to abuse others quite at his ease.'

Schleiermacher was the second celebrity that attracted Schopenhauer, and again he was destined to disappointment. He began to differ from him also after the first lecture. Schleiermacher said:

'Philosophy and Religion have the knowledge of God in common.'

'In that case,' annotes Schopenhauer, 'philosophy would have to presuppose the idea of a God; which, on the contrary, it must acquire or reject impartially according to its own development.

Schleiermacher announced that 'Philosophy and Religion cannot exist apart; no one can be a philosopher without a sense of religion. On the other hand, the religious man must study the rudiments of philosophy.'

'No one who is religious,' writes Schopenhauer, arrives as far as philosophy; he does not require it. No one who really philosophizes is religious; he walks without leading strings; his course is hazardous but unfettered.'

'This Schleiermacher is a man in a mask,' he would, say. In after years he told choice anecdotes about him, and repeatedly praised his remark that a man only learnt at the University to know what he would have to learn afterwards. The characters of Schleiermacher and Schopenhauer were too fundamentally at variance to admit of any assimilation. Schopenhauer was besides repelled by Schleiermacher's personal appearance a point on which he was extremely sensitive so that the two great men never came into immediate contact; a matter the more regrettable as Schleiermacher loved nothing so much as colloquial intercourse. Such meetings might have modified the younger man's unfairness to one who, great as are his errors, was undoubtedly the precursor of a new epoch in Protestant theology. But theology and jurisprudence were the only two branches of learning which Schopenhauer left out of regard in his studies and his writings.

His favourite professor was Heinrich August Wolf, the great Hellenist and critic, a fact that honours both master and pupil. His notes of Wolfs lectures abound in praise, while those relating to the History of Greek Antiquities are furnished with marginalia 'in Wolfs own handwriting,' as Schopenhauer appends with youthful pride at such distinction from, a revered master. It was no wonder that this philosopher, whose startling theories set the whole classical world ablaze, and whose works are justly considered models of controversial writing and refined irony, appealed to a mind that had so much in common with his own.

CHAPTER III - HIS MENTAL DEVELOPMENT

SCHOPENHAUER, like Goethe, was devoid of political enthusiasm; he pursued his studies regardless of mighty events that determined the fate of nations. These were the winter months of 1812 and 1813, when Europe throbbed with hopes of deliverance from the thraldom of Napoleon; his disastrous Russian campaign awakening and justifying these feelings. The rousing appeals to the German nation which Fichte had thundered forth with fearless energy in the winter of 1808, during the French occupation of Berlin, bore fruit now that the first chance of success dawned. Schopenhauer never mentions these addresses when he censures Fichte. Whatever views he held of his philosophy, he might have accorded a word of praise to this unflinching patriotism.

When the unsettled state of affairs after the indecisive battle of Lützen convinced Schopenhauer that this was not a likely time to receive promotion at Berlin, he merely went out of the way of these martial disturbances to meditate his inaugural dissertation. He need not be blamed for this apparent callousness any more than Goethe. Genius must be egotistic in a certain sense; it must place self-culture in the chief position; this very egotism is an element inalienable from its due development. Small and narrow spirits cannot comprehend, and therefore condemn this instinctive self-enclosure within which true genius unfolds. Schopenhauer had not Goethe's amiability to conciliate them in other ways, his was a harsh uncompromising temperament; yet he too felt he had his mission towards the world, and he must fulfill it after his bent. To say he was devoid of political enthusiasm is not to say that he was devoid of patriotism, a quality not necessarily or always free from selfish motives, as its ardent and often most egotistic admirers aver. Schopenhauer was certainly free, almost to a fault, from the weakness of national pride. His patriotism was limited to the German language, whose powerful beauties he appreciated so keenly that it maddened him to see it wielded in the clumsy grasp of ordinary writers. He was never weary of contrasting the English and French authors with those of his own country, greatly to the disadvantage of the latter. He was disgusted at the Germans' negligence of what he esteemed their only treasure. In every other point of view he was ashamed to be a German, and gladly recalled his paternal Dutch descent. Those were the days of tall talk and tiny deeds ; small wonder therefore if they met with little sympathy from a man of Schopenhauer's energetic mould. Yet in his innermost heart must surely have lurked some love of country; else why did he blame so severely in his own nation actions which he could overlook or excuse in others? Doubtless had Schopenhauer lived to witness late events he would have been as good a patriot as any.

Throughout life he hated interruptions. When therefore the tumult of war approached Berlin, Schopenhauer fled to Saxony. It took him twelve days to reach Dresden, owing to the disturbed state of the country. Ill-luck made him fall into the very midst of the army, and he was once retained as interpreter between the French and German troops, his knowledge of the former language having attained for him this unenviable distinction. He then proceeded to Weimar, but did not stay many days. Circumstances had arisen in his mother's circle that caused him to accuse her of want of fidelity to his father's memory. Whether these allegations were sufficiently proved remains doubtful; Dr. Gwinner, Schopenhauer's friend and biographer, inclines to think they were not. In any case, Schopenhauer believed them just; and they threw dark shadows over his future life, and helped yet further to separate him from his surviving parent. He retired to Rudolstadt, a charming little town in the Thuringian forest, to ponder in peace over his inaugural dissertation.

Mental work was not as easy as might be assumed from reading his flowing periods. Thought came freely enough at times ; at others it had to be secured or exhumed, and any casual noise would interrupt the thread of his reasoning. He dwells on this in the 'Parerga,' and mentions it more fully, with especial reference to his own case, in a MS. book of the Rudolstadt period.

'If I faintly perceive an idea which looks like a dim picture before me, I am possessed with an ineffable longing to grasp it; I leave everything else, and follow my idea through all its tortuous windings, as the huntsman follows the stag; I attack it from all sides and hem it in until I seize it, make it clear, and having fully mastered it, embalm it on paper. Sometimes it escapes, and then I must wait till chance discovers it to me again. Those ideas which I capture after many fruitless chases are generally the best. But if I am interrupted in one of these pursuits, especially if it be by the cry of an animal, which pierces between my thoughts, severing head from body, as by a headsman's axe, then I experience one of those pains to which we made ourselves liable when we descended into the same world as dogs, donkeys, and ducks.'

This excessive sensitiveness to noise caused Schopenhauer much suffering through life. He regarded it as a proof of mental capacity ; stoic indifference to sound was to his mind equivalent to intellectual obtuseness.

As Schopenhauer's early MS. books embodied the original foundation of those ideas which his later works merely amplified, so they are also a species of self analysis. He studied his own subjectivity, and drew his conclusions for the general out of the individual. He speaks of himself, often to himself, and thus makes us acquainted with his moral and intellectual entity.

All the thoughts which I have penned,' he says, in his MS. book 'Cogitata, 'have arisen from some external impulse, generally from a definite impression, and have been written down from this objective starting-point without a thought of their ultimate tendency. They resemble radii starting from the periphery, which all converge towards one centre, and that the fundamental thought of my doctrine; they lead to this from the most varied quarters and points of view.'

The same idea is expressed in the 'Spicilegia,' a later memorandum-book, thus proving the perfect unison of purpose that pervaded this robust life.

'My works are a succession of essays, in which I am possessed with one idea I wish to determine for its own sake by writing it down. They are put together with cement, therefore they are not shallow and dull, like the works of people who sit down to write a book page by page, according to some preconceived plan.'

The dissertation he was evolving at Rudolstadt had to be complete and symmetrical, and accordingly cost him much labour. He enjoyed the calm country atmosphere that surrounded him, its solitude was congenial, and when there were no noises he was well content. But as he lived in the Inn, where to this day a line from Horace, scratched by him on a pane, is shown to visitors, such disturbances cannot have been quite avoidable. It runs : 'Arth, Schopenhauer, majorem anni 1813 partem in hoc conclave degit. Laudaturque domus, longos quæ prospicit agros.' It seems as if there must have been an obnoxious baby on the premises, to judge from the somewhat petulant remark he wrote there :—

'It is just, though hard, that we should daily, our whole life long, hear so many babies cry, in return for having cried a few years ourselves.'

Two letters of this period are extant. They are of no intrinsic importance, but deserve quotation because they reveal Schopenhauer in an amiable and social light, after he had already acquired the character of a misanthrope. Perhaps the soothing intercourse with the pleasing scenery of Thuringia had exercised some charm even over this morose spirit, or, more likely still, Schopenhauer was at heart an amiable man, forced to put on an exterior armour of gruffness as protection from those who should have been his warmest friends, and proved his most irritating, disdainful enemies. Later the mail became a part of the man, so that *Noli me tangere* might aptly have been Schopenhauer's motto.

The first letter is undated, an habitual negligence, and characteristic, like all he did. He was the champion of Kant, who preached that time is not a real existence, but only a condition of human thought. The letters are both addressed to Frommann, the publisher and bookseller of Jena, at whose house Goethe met Minna Herzlieb, the love of his advanced age and the heroine of his 'Elective Affinities.'

'DEAR SIR,
'I must, perforce, furnish a commentary to the chapter "On the vanity of human intentions and wishes." Yesterday I feared it would rain, and today, in spite of the most beautiful weather, I am a prisoner to my room, and that because a new shoe has nearly lamed me, and would have done so quite had I gone out again today. So I am having the shoe stretched, and am holding a festival of rest and penance in honour of St. Crispin, the patron of shoemakers.

'I am only sorry that this mishap prevents me from having the pleasure of seeing you and your charming family. Professor Oken has kindly sent me some books, with which I pass my time agreeably. I have everything I need, and I sincerely hope that you will not allow my being here to disturb your plans. I only let you know because I wish to ask you to tell Herr von Altenburg, who seeks a travelling companion through this neighbourhood, that I shall be happy to accompany him, if it suits him to go to-morrow evening.

'Please remember me to your family, and believe me sincerely yours,

'ARTHUR SCHOPENHAUER.'

Meanwhile Schopenhauer's first work was completed, and sent in to the University of Jena, which bestowed on him the too-often abused title of Doctor of Philosophy. This, 'Die Vierfache Wurzel des Satzes vom Zureichenden Grunde,' already contained the germs of his entire philosophy.

This little tractate, On the Quadruple Root of the Doctrine of Adequate Cause, is intended to show that the idea of causality is not grounded upon a single axiom or necessary truth, but upon four, or rather perhaps upon one necessary truth contemplated in a fourfold aspect, according to its relation to any one in particular of the four classes comprising, in Schopenhauer's words, everything capable of being regarded by us as an object, i.e.., the entire compass of our ideas. These are respectively: Phenomena, or the objects of sensuous perception ; Reason, or the objects of rational perception ; Being, under the categories of space and time ; and the Will. Schopenhauer investigates each class separately, and endeavours to show that the doctrine of causality, in its relation to each, assumes a different aspect. Hence it ensues that 'the necessity which accompanies a proposition conceived as demonstrable *a priori* is not one and invariable, but as manifold as the sources of the proposition itself.' The little essay, which, notwithstanding the abstruseness of the subject, is written in a clear and lively style, is remarkable for the stress already laid upon the idea of Will, and for its hints of the applicability of the author's metaphysical theories to ethical and aesthetic criticism.

'Rudolstadt, 4th November, 1813.
'DEAR MR. FROMMANN,
I send you the treatise for which I have taken my degree, and at the same time return you ' Hegel's Logic' with many thanks. I should not have kept the book so long had I not felt sure that you would read it as little as I. But I should not yet like to part from the other philosopher, Francis Bacon ; may I keep the book a little longer ? unless of course you require it. In any case you shall have it back in a few weeks. I sincerely hope that you have not suffered much through the war, and that no domestic sorrow disturbs the joy which you doubtless feel at the happy progress of the cause of Germany and mankind. Next week I purpose to take up my abode again in Weimar.

'Remember me to your family, and believe me faithfully yours,

'ARTHUR SCHOPENHAUER.'

On his arrival at Weimar he presented his mother with a copy of his work. She did not even evince the ordinary interest of an acquaintance, still less that of a mother, for her son's production, of however uncongenial a character.

'The fourfold root,' she said. 'Oh, I suppose that is a book for apothecaries.'

His haughty reply is surely pardonable.

'It will be read, mother, when even the lumber room will not contain a copy of your works.'

It was diamond cut diamond. 'The whole edition of yours will still be on hand,' she answered.

Both prophecies were fulfilled in due course. The greater portion of Schopenhauer's first edition became waste paper, while his mother's works were eagerly read. For years nothing irritated Arthur more than the question : 'Are you the son of the famous Johanna Schopenhauer?' But as time went on her fame paled before his; her works and travels were forgotten; the present generation hardly knows of their existence. Before his death she was merely the mother of her son.

This scene did not lessen the breach between them, which during that winter spent in Weimar many things helped to widen. Johanna Schopenhauer was extravagant; and Arthur feared, not without reason, that she was squandering his patrimony. He had a nervous dread of being left without the means of a comfortable existence, for he discerned his own inability to earn money. This led to violent altercations, so that it became more and more impossible for them to live together. In the spring they parted, with bitter feelings on either side.

Schopenhauer has been much blamed for his want of filial piety to his mother ; it is undeniable that he could not make sufficient allowance for idiosyncrasies foreign to himself, yet much can be said in his defence. It has been justly remarked that in Catholic countries the relations between parents and children are looked on as the most sacred, while in Protestant lands those of husband and wife take the foremost place. Though Germany is largely Protestant, this Catholic trait has taken deep root, whence Arthur Schopenhauer was censured for a step which would require no apology in this country, where sons are under no necessity, like daughters, of suffering more uncongenial parental intercourse than they choose. 'Love for a mother is the holiest thing on earth,' says one of the admirers of his philosophy, who blames him in this respect. But abstract phrases such as these are ill calculated to be decisive in particular cases. Kant's categorical imperative has proved most mischievous in its too universal adoption in the domain of ethics. 'Thou shalt,' is daily preached and taught, regardless of the enormous influence circumstances, character, and position exercise in denning the status of right and wrong in individual cases. It metes but one measure to all men. It is incontestable that a son should reverence his mother; when love and sympathy exist between them this reverence will never be wanting. But the very thing which gives family life its charm, the natural bond which knits parents and children together, turns all its sweetness into bitter gall if these essentials are wanting. Throughout life too little stress is laid upon the consideration that persons who would never have chosen each other as friends, are often forced to live with each other in the closest, and therefore the most irritating relationship; with characters so antagonistic, that the very person of the one may jar to the point of actual suffering upon the nerves of the other. Nor is this one of the trials that grow more bearable from force of habit; distinctly the reverse. Every day of such jarring intercourse makes the relationship more intolerable to the sensitive party. This was the case with Schopenhauer.

'You and I are two,' he exclaimed occasionally, from the depths of his being, untuned by these scenes.

The want of affinity between mother and son was the fault of neither party, but it is certainly strange that Madame Schopenhauer could not think more highly of his immense genius, which Goethe, and others whom she honoured, discerned at a glance.

This winter had its compensations, however, as well as its troubles. In the *salon* of his mother Schopenhauer met many famous men, whose intercourse was pleasure and interest sufficient to retain him longer in the place than he had originally intended; for though he liked the little capital, he found its social demands too distracting for calm, philosophical thought. Foremost among all, Goethe attracted him. When his majestic form appeared in Madame Schopenhauer's drawing-room, her son had eye and ear for no one else. They must have met before, probably at Weimar, certainly at Jena, as an anecdote on record proves. It was at a party there : some girls were making fun of a young doctor of philosophy, who had retired alone into a window-niche, looking severe, and evidently absorbed in thought, while the rest of the company were assembled round the tea-table. An elderly, noble-looking man went up to the giggling girls, and asked the cause of their mirth.

'Children,' said Goethe reprovingly, 'leave that youth in peace; in due time he will grow over all our heads.'

The 'Vierfache Wurzel' entirely won Goethe's interest. His open mind recognised the value of the treatise, and though its fundamental tendencies were diametrically opposed to his own, it yet contained many passages that expressed his ideas. Besides, Goethe always hailed with pleasure the advent of that *rara avis,* an independent thinker. This fell in the time when the poet was least approachable. He had been giving his attention to Science, and had met with cold rebuffs and sneers ; the value of his discoveries was not tested, because the specialists mistrusted the amateur. On the subject of his Colour Studies, he was childishly sensitive, to the point of saying to Eckermann: 'As to what I have done as a poet, I take no pride in it whatever. Excellent poets have lived at the same time with myself; more excellent poets have lived before me and will come after me. But that in my century I am the only person who knows the truth in the difficult science of colours of that, I say, I am not a little proud.'

Perceiving Schopenhauer's independent mind, he placed his theory before the youth forty years his junior. Private theatricals were being enacted at Madame Schopenhauer's. Adele Schopenhauer, ten years younger than her brother, was playing a boy's part, dressed in the white brocaded coat Goethe wore when taking his degree at Strasburg. Goethe invited Arthur to spend the next evening quietly at his house. That evening Schopenhauer felt the whole height and depth of the marvellous genius, whom he never ceased to admire.

'Goethe educated me anew,' he said, and indeed, excepting Schiller, there was no one to whom this mighty spirit became so stimulating, or on whom his influence proved so beneficial. Goethe, though attracted to Schopenhauer, thought him 'hard to know.' The benefits of intercourse remained one-sided; the poet never inclined greatly to philosophy, and was too wedded to habits of thought to imbibe a new system. He continued to manifest a lively interest, but Schopenhauer suspected on good grounds that he never thoroughly read his later works.

Schopenhauer was naturally flattered at Goethe's proposal that he should investigate his despised and beloved theory of colours, and his interest was soon aroused. Goethe sent him his own optical apparatus, and instruments, in order that the young man might test the matter for himself, and at leisure. Schopenhauer spared no pains ; he entered with all the ardour of a disciple, inclined to grant the blind subservience Goethe demanded in later life. But presently he refused the elder's leading strings, venturing to differ and oppose on closer investigation. A pamphlet *Ueber das Sehen und die Farben* was the result, received by Goethe with mixed feelings. Schopenhauer preserved a warm interest in the subject. In 1840, hearing that Sir Charles Eastlake was about to translate Goethe's work into English, he addressed to him in the same language the following characteristic letter:

'SIR, Allow me to hail and to cheer you as the propagator of the true theory of colours into England, and the translator of the work, which occupied its author's thoughts during all his lifetime, far more than all his poetry, as his biography and memoirs amply testify.

'As to myself I am Goethe's personal scholar and first publicly avowed proselyte in the theory of colours. In the year 1813 and 1814 he instructed me personally, lent me the greater part of his own apparatus, and exhibited the more compound and difficult experiments himself to me. Accordingly you will find me mentioned in his "*Tag und Jahreshefte*" under the year 1816 and 1819. If you should wish a more extensive and new account of me, it is to be found in the twelfth volume of the new edition of Kant's works, edited by Schubert and Rosenkranz. I am a metaphysician of Kant's school.

'Indeed, Sir, I have not seen your translation, but only know it by two reviews, one in the "[[Edinburgh Review]]," and the other in the "Athenæum." But I am convinced of its correctness by the testimony of the Scotch reviewer, who, though a professed enemy of your undertaking, declares the translation to be one of the best ever made from the German. And as for the rest, that most malignant, impertinent, and insolent piece of criticism ought to encourage you, as you plainly perceive the inward rage, deep hatred and rancour so ill-concealed behind his affected cool contempt of the great man's work. He inwardly feels that the detection of an immense shameful error is approaching, and accordingly we see Newtonianism behaving like a tiger attacked in its own den. The review in the "Athenæum" is a most pitiful performance: it coincides with the other in taking for granted beforehand that Goethe must be wrong, is wrong, and cannot but be wrong. These fools have never impartially examined the controversy, because they would never allow themselves to doubt, only for a moment, the truth of the Newtonian creed, lest their faith might be shaken. They cling to the palpable lie of colours, and to that of unequal refrangibility, though every achromatic opera-glass is a refutation of the latter. But they feel a secret misgiving, for all their bragging" and insolence. At them now!

I regret two things: (1.) That you did not translate the polemical part, but only gave extracts of it: this part is most essential, as it shows the gross manner in which Newton, by his clumsy experiments, imposed upon himself and others : translate it, for God's sake, or better Goethe's, if your translation should see a second edition. (2.) That you did not express a firm conviction of Goethe's truth and Newton's error: I hope that this is more a want of courage than of insight into the truth. By the " Edinburgh Review" I conceive that you are a painter, and as such you are awed into some respect before those renowned natural philosophers and mathematicians, the Brewsters and the Whewells and the Devils. I see I must rouse your courage a little by setting up authority against authority. Well, Sir, what I am now going to state, I affirm upon my honour, my conscience, and my oath, to be exactly true. In the year 1830, as I was going to publish in Latin the same treatise which in German accompanies this letter, I went to Dr. Seebeck, of the Berlin Academy, who is universally admitted to be the first natural philosopher (in. the English sense of the word meaning Physiker) of Germany; he is the discoverer of thermo-electricity and of several physical truths. I questioned him on his opinion on the controversy between Goethe and Newton: he was extremely cautious, made me promise that I should not print and publish anything of what he might say, and at last, being hard pressed by me, he confessed that indeed Goethe was perfectly right and Newton wrong; but that he had no business to tell the world so. He died since, the old coward. Truth has a hard stand and a difficult progress in this vile world: in England, moreover, they take this matter as a national affair; however silly this may be. We must display some courage on our side, and not suffer ourselves to be intimidated. My great master being dead, I must do whatever I can to uphold the standard of true Chromatology, which you have raised in the very country of the enemy, to my utmost joy and delight.

'Please, Sir, do peruse the little treatise, which I take the liberty of sending you along with this letter, by means of a commercial traveller; and pray, do not judge of its importance by its bulk. It contains the only and for ever true theory of physiological colour, a theory which would be true even if Goethe was wrong: it does not depend on his positions. The main point is exposed in par. 5, which however cannot be rightly understood, nor properly appreciated, without having read what goes before. My style is very perspicuous and easy, so you will read it with the utmost facility. And afterwards if, bearing in mind the numerical fractions (of the activity of the retina) by which I express the chief six colours, you contemplate these colours singly, then you will find that only by this, and by no other theory upon earth, you come to understand the peculiar sensation which every colour produces in your eye, and thereby get an insight into the very essence of every colour, and of colour in general.

'Likewise my theory alone gives the true sense in which the notion of complementary colours is to be taken, viz. as having no reference to *light*, but to the retina, and not being a redintegration of white light, but of the full action of the *retina*, which by every colour undergoes a bipartition

either in yellow and violet,

3/4 1/4

or in orange and blue,

2/3 1/3

or in red and green.

1/2 1/2

This is in short the great mystery.

'Some unbiased persons have acknowledged that I found out the main point of all Chromatology. But if Goethe, notwithstanding all his glory, could not overcome prejudice and German dullness, how could I, that am only known among metaphysicians. However my theory is taught as the true one, and as containing the main point, to which Goethe's is a sequel, in "Pierer's Keal-lexicon der Medicinischen Wissenschaften," and even in that vulgar[2] but widely circulated dictionary, "Conversations-lexicon," you find stated under the head "Farbe," that I ought to be read along with Goethe as most essential.

'May the force of truth, Sir, enlighten your mind,, and induce you to translate also this little treatise of mine, or at least to make an extract of it for the English public! This is my most fervent desire. But if you should determine to do it, I wish you would compare the Latin edition of this my treatise, contained in the third volume of "Scriptores ophth. min. ed. Justus Radius, 1830" under the title "Theoria &c." I am sorry I cannot send it you, being only possessed of a single copy, which I cannot part with, and would be obliged to purchase the whole three volumes in order to get it, moreover, I am not sure that you understand Latin. However, you may easily find the aforesaid Scriptores in any medical library in London, especially at the oculists. Besides, when it appeared in 1830, I sent copies of my treatise in Latin to Sir Everard Home, the Professor Jameson in Edinburgh, and to Dr. Michael Kyan in London. Perhaps you might get one of them. It is no exact translation of the German treatise, but somewhat altered in the form, and also a little shortened; but materially the content is the same : only it is improved in some explanations, especially in the demonstration of the utter impossibility of Newton's theory, and of the falsehood of the explanation of physiological colours given by Charles Scherffer, 1761, and repeated ever since, even by Cuvier. A translation of the German treatise as it is would always be sufficient for the main point and purpose. I cancel some passages in the copy I send you, not as false, but as trifling. As my theory is entirely physiological, taking colour merely as a sensation, and with respect to the eyes it is the primary theory, and anterior to all explications of the outward causes of that sensation, which are the physical and chemical colours.

'If ever I can be of any use to you in forwarding the great object of true Chromatology, you will always find me ready for it, and, I hardly need say so, without the least interested motive, nor expecting any retribution for whatever trouble I might take, as I am an independent gentleman, living on my fortune and not by my pen.

ARTHUR SCHOPENHAUER

'Dr. Schopenhauer has a mighty head,' said Goethe, but he evidently did not feel quite at his ease with Arthur. His morose views jarred on the elder's joyous nature.

Willst du dich des Lebens freuen,

So musst der Welt du Werth verleihen.

he wrote in Schopenhauer's album on parting. Quoting Chamfort, Schopenhauer wrote in the margin:

'Il vaut mieux laisser les hommes pour ce qu'ils sont, que les prendre pour ce qu'ils ne sont pas ; 'adding on his own part, 'Eien de si riche qu'un grand soi-meme.'

Goethe had fathomed his young friend's disposition; Schopenhauer in return had formed his opinion of the poet. 'That Goethe was an egotist is most true.' He severely censured Goethe's courtier life, and considered that he had squandered his best years and strength for the sake of outward show. He judged Goethe by himself, and believed that he would have gained in depth and breadth of thought had he led a more solitary introspective life. The subject is open to question ; emphatically Schopenhauer himself would have been as much out of place at Court as Raphael Hythloday in any but an Utopian Kingdom.

The two spent many pleasant evenings together discussing ethics and aesthetics. Schopenhauer complains of Goethe's deep-rooted realism, which only permitted him to see things from that point of view, so that these conversations generally ended in friendly disagreement. Frederick

Mayer also contributed greatly towards rendering Weimar interesting to Schopenhauer. He introduced him to Indian lore, a study traceable throughout all his writings, deeply imbued with the spirit of Buddhism. Everything that interested him he pursued with a passionate ardour hardly appropriate to an analytical philosopher. A play could move him to an intense degree. A performance of Calderon's 'Constant Prince' so affected him he was forced to quit an evening party at his mother's and retire to solitude.

Besides the persons mentioned, a woman exercised an immense fascination over Schopenhauer in this Weimar period. This was Caroline Jaegemann, prima donna and leading actress at the Court Theatre, whose rare beauty, voice and delivery has remained traditional for all that is perfect and entrancing in dramatic art. She was the Mrs. Siddons of the German stage, and her power was so mighty that even Goethe had to retire before it, and give up the management of the theatre when their opinions clashed. She was in these days the recognised mistress of the Duke Carl August, who endowed her with the title and estates of Heigendorf, whither she retired after his death. Schopenhauer was completely enraptured with the actress.

'I would have married this woman,' he once said to his mother, 'even if I had only seen her breaking stones on the high road.'

His infatuation is the more extraordinary as she was not of the type irresistible to him. He was very susceptible to female charms, but it was slender brunettes whom he found dangerous. Caroline Jaegemann, on the contrary, was short and fair, but the antique mould in which her wonderful beauty was cast probably induced him into a deviation from his usual canons of taste.

These things combined made Weimar a distracting and unfruitful residence. He could not philosophise calmly among so much outer excitement. He must break from these syren charms before they overwhelmed him. Having preserved a pleasant recollection of Dresden from former visits he removed thither in the spring of 1814.

'A good store of resignation is a most necessary provision for the journey of life,' he writes at this period. 'It must be first abstracted from disappointed hopes, and the sooner the better for the rest of the journey.'

Another extract from his notebook also speaks of inward conflicts, such as more or less keenly every highly gifted nature, which enters life with ideal aspirations and discovers its dreary realities, must fight.

' A child has no conception of the inexorableness of natural laws and the inflexible persistency of everything to its own entity. The child thinks even lifeless things will bend a little to its will, because he feels himself at one with Nature, or because he believes it friendly towards him, through ignorance of the spirit of the world. As a child I once threw my shoe into a large bowl of milk and was discovered entreating it to jump out again. A child must also learn to know the malignity of animals before he will beware of them. It is only after mature experience that we realise the inflexibility of human characters, which no entreaties, no reasoning, no examples, no benefits can change: how on the contrary every human being follows out his own manner of action, his own way of thought and his own capabilities with the unerringness of a natural law, so that whatever you try to effect, he will remain unchanged. When we have felt and seen this clearly we at last cease our attempts to change people and form them according to our wish : we learn to bear with those whom we cannot dispense with, and to keep those at a distance with whom we have nothing in common.

'Note this, my soul, once for all, and be wise. Man is subjective, not objective, subjective throughout. If you had a dog, and wished to attach him to you, would you reason like this: The animal must at least perceive one of my numerous rare and excellent qualities and that will suffice to make him devoted to me for ever. If you thought thus you would be a fool. Stroke it, feed it, and then be what you will, it will not care but will grow faithfully attached to you. Now remember, it is just the same with human beings, that is why Goethe says: "*denn ein erbärmlicher Schuft, so wie der Mensch, ist der Hund.*" (For a dog is a miserable rascal like man.) This is why miserable fools so often succeed in life ; they are nothing in themselves, nothing by themselves, nothing absolute ; their whole being is relative, and for other people ; they are always means, never ends, mere baits. (All this is expressed with great euphemism in that line of Sophocles : *Xapis Xapiv yap eotiv n tixtovo ael.* Ajax, 517.) Nor do I admit of any exceptions from this rule, at least no complete exceptions ; there are certainly some very few people who have objective moments in their lives, but I doubt whether they attain to greater heights than this. Now do not except yourself; examine your loves, your friendships, see whether your objective opinions be not mostly subjective ones in disguise; try whether you can thoroughly appreciate the good qualities of those who do not like you, and so forth, and then be tolerant, it is your bounden duty. And as you are all so subjective learn to understand your own weakness. As you know that you only like a man who is friendly towards you, and that he only continues thus if you show yourself amiable towards him, be so: from out this feigned friendship a true one will gradually ripen. Your own weakness and subjectivity need to be deceived. —This is really a deduction from politeness; but I could reason from a much deeper source.'

CHAPTER IV - HIS LIFE AT DRESDEN

THUS at variance with himself, discontented, craving both for solitude and human sympathy, Schopenhauer took up his residence at Dresden. His genius was fermenting within him ; this was the *Sturm und Drang* period of his life, he was tossed hither and thither by conflicting desires, through which however, steadily and surely, the master passion forced itself into prominence. From his first dawn of thought he had felt in discord with the world ; a feeling that caused him uneasiness in youth, since he feared the majority must be in the right. *Vox populi, vox Dei*. The study of Helvetius first cheered and upheld him. Then by slow degrees his own great mind mellowed to ripeness and he needed the world less because he had obtained *un grand soimême*. He grew satisfied to enjoy 'the solitude of Kings.'

But this was later : when he removed to Dresden the conflict was raging with full force, as extracts from his notebooks prove. These notebooks, continued from his University days, show us the man Schopenhauer in his remarkable individuality, besides containing all the genius and elements that went up to make his principal work *Die Welt als Wille und Vorstellung*.' He had not been long at Dresden before he wrote :

'Whenever I first enter a new condition of life, or come among fresh surroundings, I am dissatisfied and irritable. This arises because I had surveyed all the bearings of this new condition beforehand by the aid of reason ; while now the actual present, full of new objects, acts more powerfully upon me than usual, and is yet withal deficient, as the present must be, because I demand from it the fulfilment of all that this new condition had promised. Its vivid impressions compel me to occupy myself with present details, which hinder me from attaining a complete survey. Too intense a life in the present is a source of much vexation to me and to all excitable people. Those who are chiefly guided by Reason (more especially as applied to practical ends), those truly reasonable, well-balanced, even tempered characters are far more cheerful minded, though less prone to elation and sudden moods of brilliancy ; neither have they a spark of originality. For their lives are rooted and grounded in received impressions, and life itself and the present stand out in faint colours to their view. Those in whom Reason is the chief force, (just because the other forces are not strong) the purely rational, cannot endure much solitude, though they are not lively in society. That which they have apprehended satisfies but a part of their nature, they need impressions, and these must be sought for in reality. Whereas people gifted with a vivid imagination perceive sufficient by its help and can more easily dispense with reality and society.'

Schopenhauer had early discerned that his peculiar temperament made it unlikely that he should find many friends ; but in those Dresden days he still frequented society. He did not regard the possession of friends as any proof of worth, rather the reverse. He writes :

' Nothing manifests more ignorance of human nature than to adduce the number of a man's friends as a proof of his desert : as if men bestowed their friendship according to desert. As if they were not rather like dogs who love anyone that stroke them or throws them a bone and take no further notice of them. He who best understands how to caress them, be they the vilest curs, he has the most friends.

'On the contrary it may be asserted that men of much intellectual worth, more especially if they have genius, can have but few friends. Their clear-sighted eye soon discovers all faults, and their just perception is repelled afresh by the enormity of these failings. Nothing but the utmost necessity can force them to conceal this feeling. Men of genius can only be personally beloved by many (leaving reverence for authority out of the question) when the gods grant them perennial cheerfulness, a gaze embellishing all it rests upon ; or if they have been led gradually to take men as they are, that is, to treat fools according to their folly.'

This all embellishing power was foreign to Schopenhauer, he was forced to seek compensation elsewhere; he found it in cognition. He did not say, like Troilus,

I will not be myself, nor have cognition

Of what I feel;

he sought it ardently, he made it the keystone of the arch, the fulcrum of his system.

'My life is a bitter-sweet draught ; like my whole being it is a constant gleaning of cognition, an acquisition of knowledge regarding this actual world and my relation to it. The result of this cognition is sad and depressing ; but this state of cognisance, this gain of insight, this penetration of truth, is thoroughly pleasureable, and strange to say, mixes sweet with bitter.'

Just before quitting Weimar he wrote :

'How is it possible for a man to be content till he has arrived at complete concord with himself ? As long as two voices speak within him by turns, whatever pleases the one will dissatisfy the other, and therefore one will always murmur. But has there ever been a man in complete accord with himself ? Nay, is not the very thought a paradox ? '

To this he added some months later :

'The desire of most philosophers that man should attain complete accord, and be at unison with himself, is impossible and self-contradictory. For as a man, inner discord is his lot as long as he lives. He can be only one thing thoroughly, but he has the capacity, the indestructible possibility within him of being everything else. If he has decided for one thing, all the other capacities remain in readiness, and clamour constantly to emerge from possibility into reality : he must constantly repress them, conquer them, kill them, as long as he wishes to be that one thing. For instance, he may choose to think, and not act or work, but the power of work and action cannot be suddenly eradicated. As long as he lives as thinker, he must hour by hour constantly destroy the active man within him and fight eternally with himself, as with a monster whose heads grow again as fast as they are hewn off. If he choose sanctity, he must continue to destroy his sensual being all his life long ; he cannot do so once for all ; his sensual self will live as long as he. If he has decided for enjoyment in whatever form, then he must struggle all his life long with himself as with a being that longs to be pure, free and holy, for lie has not lost the possibility of being this ; it must be hourly uprooted. Thus it is with everything in endless modifications. Now one capacity and now another may conquer, man remains the wrestling ground. The one may be continually victorious, still the other struggles continually, for it must live as long as himself. A human being is the possibility of many contradictions.

'How then could unity be possible ? It exists neither in saint or villain ; or rather no such thing as a saint or villain is possible. For they are alike men ; unquiet beings, combatants, gladiators in the arena of life.

'Surely it is good he should distinguish the capacity whose defeat pains him most, and allow this to be always victorious, which is possible by the aid of ever present reason. Let him resign himself cheerfully to the pain caused by defeat of the antagonist's tendency. So he evolves character. For the battle of life cannot be fought without pain, may not end without bloodshed ; man must bear the pain in every case, for he is conquered as well as conqueror. *Hæc est vivendi conditio.*'

Indeed, long before this period, Schopenhauer had applied to himself Chamfort's axiom : *Il y a une prudence superieure a celle qu'on qualifie ordinairement de ce nom, elle consiste a suivre hardiment son caractere, en acceptant avec courage les desavantages et les inconvenients qu'il faut produire.* He knew he had genius, that he was no ordinary man, and he acknowledged it with his habitual sincerity of speech. He weighed his duties towards the world in the balance with the weight and the intensity of his natural gifts ; and he came to the conclusion, that 'a man gifted with genius, by merely being and working, sacrifices himself for all mankind ; therefore he is free from the obligation of sacrificing himself in particular to individuals. On this account, he may ignore many claims which others are bound to fulfil. He still suffers and achieves more than all the rest.'

Schopenhauer has been accused of vanity, of presumption, and of the pride of intellect. In a measure these accusations are just, but they are not wholly so, nor are Schopenhauer's faults incapable of palliation. Perhaps nothing is more absurd and pitiable than the commonly accepted definition of modesty. 'If it were not my own,' says a man, 'I would praise it,' speaking of something which is the handywork of another, and which his purse alone has permitted him to buy. He feigns to believe that his possession of the object detracts from its worth. The same with genius or talent of any kind. The possessor is to be unconscious, clamours the multitude ; in other words, only thus by silence will it tolerate even the smallest elevation above the average. The Philistines would mow humanity like grass, bringing it all to one level, then none would uprear their heads, all might be content ; envy, hatred and malice abolished, the lion lie down with the lamb, the millennium dawn. Genius feels mentally lonely, he finds it impossible to amalgamate with the average, he is forced to perceive that he is in some manner different. So he scrutinizes, 'Am I lower than the rest or higher?' The very keenness of perception, which the world is ready enough to praise when applied to objective matters, gives him clear-sightedness. Then 'Oh vanity!' cries the world.

Schopenhauer refused to believe that a man could be ignorant of his powers, any more than he could fail to know whether his height were above or below the average. It was absurd, he deemed, to imagine that one could have a great mind without knowing it. He, for his part, always suspected that self-depreciating celebrities were in the right. He rather held with Corneille :—

La fausse humilite ne met plus en credit ;

Je sais ce que je vaux et crois ce qu'on ra'en dit.

In his later years Schopenhauer undoubtedly became vain in the worst sense of the word ; in these earlier years he merely took his own measure and estimated his inborn powers, regarding them as a talent entrusted to his keeping for the world. Can a man be accused of intellectual pride who could deem an uncultured noble mind superior to Bacon with all his learning and power?

'Though wanting all intellectual advantages and culture, a noble character stands forth boldly, and is not deficient in anything. The greatest genius, on the other hand, will excite disapprobation if stained with moral defects. As torches and fireworks pale before the sun, even so are intellect, genius, and beauty outshone and obscured by goodness of heart. Wherever it appears in a high degree, it more than compensates for the want of these qualities ; nay, we are ashamed to feel that we miss them. The narrowest intellect, the most grotesque ugliness, if allied to this rare nobleness of soul, are transfigured, irradiated by beauty of a higher kind, wisdom speaks out of them that strikes all others dumb. Moral goodness is a transcendental quality, belongs to an order of things which reaches above this life and is incommensurable with any other perfection. Where it is present in a high degree it widens the heart until it embraces the world, and everything lies within and nothing without, because it identifies all being with its own. . . . What are wit and genius ; what Bacon, when compared to this?'

Schopenhauer knew he was different to the mass, and constantly repeated to himself that he was a stranger. 'It must be lonely on the heights.' The higher a man stood mentally, the lower must his fellow-men appear. He was not a misanthrope, he merely despised men ; καταφρονάνϑρωπος, not μιοάνϑρωπος, was the distinction he himself drew.

'I read in the face of the Apollo Belvedere the just and deep displeasure felt by the god of the Muses for the wretched and incorrigible obstinacy of the Philistines. At them he aimed his arrows ; he wished to destroy the brood of the eternally mawkish.'

He was penetrated with the conviction that he had been placed in a world peopled with beings morally and intellectually contemptible, from whom he must keep apart, seeking out the few better ones to honour and value, and making it his duty to instruct the others and raise them from their debased condition. For this end he required leisure to think and work, and this leisure was his, thanks to his competence which raised him above the necessity of gaining his daily bread. He could live wholly for his bent. 'Never forget, my friend,' he says to himself, 'that you are a philosopher, called by Nature thereto and to nothing else. Never tread the paths of the Philistines, for even were you desirous to become one, it could not be, you would remain a half-Philistine and a failure.'

'In order that man may preserve a lofty frame of mind, turning his thoughts from the temporal to the eternal ; in one word, to keep a higher consciousness alive in him ; pain, suffering, and failure are as needful as ballast to a ship, without which it does not draw enough water, becomes a plaything for the winds and waves, travels no certain road, and easily overturns.'

'Suffering is a condition of the efficacy of genius. Do you believe that Shakespeare and Goethe would have written, Plato philosophised, Kant criticised Pure Reason, if they had found satisfaction and contentment in the actual world surrounding them ; if they had felt at home in it, and it had fulfilled their desires?'

Schopenhauer's first task on his removal to Dresden was to complete the pamphlet on colours for Goethe. He then began to work at his own philosophical system with energy and ardour. As isolated thoughts came, he jotted them down. A marginal note, dated 1849, says of these memoranda :

'These sheets, written at Dresden during the years 1814 to 1818, show the fermenting process of my thoughts, out of which my whole philosophy evolved, revealing itself by degrees, like a beautiful landscape out of a morning mist. It is worthy of notice that already in 1814 (my twenty-seventh year) all the dogmas of my system, even the subordinate, were established.'

His state of mind during these years of fermentation is best told in his own words.

'A work forms itself under my hands, or rather in my mind, a philosophy uniting ethics and metaphysics, which till now have been as wrongly dissociated as men have been separated into body and soul. The work grows, takes substance gradually and slowly, like the child in the womb. I do not know what originated first, what last. I discern one member, one vessel, one part after another ; that is to say, I write them down without troubling myself about the unity of the whole, for I know that all has sprung from one source. Thus arises an organic whole, and only such an one can live.

'I who sit here, who am known by my friends, I comprehend the development of my work as little as the mother does that of the child within her womb. I behold it, and say, like the mother, "I am blessed with the hope of offspring." My mind draws nourishment from the outer world by means of reason and sense ; this nourishment gives shape to my work, but I know not how, nor why, this happens to me and not to another who has this nourishment also.

'Chance, supreme ruler of this world of sense, grant me life and peace but a few years more. I love my work as the mother loves her child. When it is ready, when it is born, use your right, claim interest for delay. Yet should I succumb sooner in this iron age, then may these immature attempts, these studies, be given to the world as they are ; perchance there may arise some kindred spirit who will understand how to piece the fragments and restore the antique.'

He did not seclude himself; on the contrary, he sought society more eagerly than usual. He was constantly to be seen in the many rich art galleries of Dresden. Raphael's divine Madonna di S. Sisto was his especial favourite ; he has written some lines on it that wonderfully characterise the strange, startled, rapt expression in the eye of the child Jesus.

Sie trägt zur Welt ihn, und er schaut entsetzt

In ihrer Gräu'l chaotische Verwirrung,

In ihres Tobens wilde Raserei,

In ihres Treibens nie geheilte Thorheit ;

In ihrer Quaalen nie gestillten Schmerz,

Entsetzt : doch strahlet Ruh', und Zuversicht,

Und Siegesglanz sein Aug', verkündigend

Schon der Erlösung ewige Gewissheit.

His evenings were spent with friends or at the theatre, of which Schopenhauer was always a great admirer, as well as an acute critic. 'Who does not visit the theatre,' he says, 'resembles one who dresses without looking at himself in the glass.' 'Dramatic art can only affect at the moment ;

therefore no artistic pleasure is rarer, for it can only be obtained by the actual presence of a man of great talent. Other arts, whose triumphs are durable, have always something to exhibit ; the drama very seldom ; nay rather it shows most garishly man's incapacity for attaining excellence.'

After hearing Don Giovanni, he noted, 'Don Giovanni is the most vivid illustration how life is ύπουλος.' He often quoted, with great satisfaction, a criticism Goethe had spoken on the opera. According to him, the merriment in Don Giovanni was only surface deep, while a serious groundwork forms the basis of the play; and the music is a just expression of this double life.

Schopenhauer might be seen sitting for hours before some picture. 'You must treat a work of art,' he said, 'like a great man ; stand before it and wait patiently till it deigns to speak.' His views on art are contained in the chapter 'On the Metaphysics of the Beautiful and the Esthetic' (Parerga).

The charming country around Dresden was an additional attraction to Schopenhauer. He loved Nature, and found support and inspiration in communion with her. To his life's end he walked with an energetic hurried step ; in these youthful days his massive square figure tearing along the banks of the Elbe, pausing occasionally to jot down a thought, was a familiar object to the good people of Dresden. He did not love these people any more than the Germans as a whole. 'The North Saxon,' he said, 'is clumsy without being awkward; and the South Saxon awkward without being clumsy.'

Another of his favourite thinking places was the large conservatory in the Zwinger. At times the divine afflatus would so ferment in him that his looks and gestures resembled a maniac's. Once, lost in thought, he was striding up and down before the plants whose physiognomy he was studying, asking himself whence they had these varied shapes and colours. 'What would these shrubs reveal to me by their curious forms? What is the inner subjective being, the Will, that manifests itself in these leaves and flowers?' He must have spoken aloud, and by this, and his violent gesticulations attracted the notice of the keeper, who felt curious as to who this eccentric gentleman could be. Going up as Schopenhauer was leaving the conservatory, he asked him who he was. 'Yes, if you could tell me who I am, I should be greatly indebted,' answered Schopenhauer. The man stared in blank amazement, and was confirmed in his suspicions of the stranger's insanity.

Another day he had paced the orangery, then in full bloom. Having secured a thought he had long wrestled for, he rushed home intoxicated with joy. Some of the blossoms had fallen on to his coat. 'You are in blossom, sir,' said his landlady, picking them off. 'Of course I am,' he replied to her in no small bewilderment, 'how should the trees bear fruit if they did not blossom?'

As his work progressed and his own views evolved before his mental vision, his pessimism grew confirmed. He was naturally nervous, σύσκολος. Whenever the postman brought a letter he would start at the thought of possible evil. He confessed, 'If I have nothing that alarms me I grow alarmed at this very condition, as if there must still be something of which I am only ignorant for a time. "Misera conditio nostra."' At the outbreak of the wars of liberation he was pursued with the fear of being forced to serve. He was easily angered, suspicious and irritable. 'Its safer trusting fear than faith,' was one of his favourite quotations. As a child of six he had once persuaded himself that he was abandoned by his parents, and was found in a passion of tears on their return from a long walk. The slightest noise at night made him start and seize the pistols that always lay ready loaded. He would never trust himself under the razor of a barber, and he fled from the mere mention of an infectious disease. He carried a little leathern drinking-cup about with him if he dined in a public place, to avoid possible contagion, and his pipes and cigar tips were carefully locked away after use lest another person should touch them. Accounts or any notes regarding his property were never entrusted to the German language ; his expenses, were written in English, his business affairs in Greek or Latin. His valuables were hidden in the strangest places, he even labelled them with deceptive names to avert the suspicion of thieves, thus, his coupons as 'Arcana medica.' He hid bonds among old letters, and gold under his inkstand. This inborn nervousness caused him much torture, and was bitterly regretted, but appears to have been quite unconquerable. All this of course seems extremely petty and contemptible, unworthy a philosopher. Alas, man is at best 'all with speckles pied.'

Schopenhauer himself says : 'Persons of wit and genius, and all such with whom the cultivation of their intellectual, theoretical, and mental paths has outsped that of their moral and practical character, are often not only awkward and laughable in real life, as Plato has noted in the 7th book of the Republic, and Goethe has depicted in Tasso, but also morally weak, despicable, ay even bad.'

Concerning his pessimistic doctrines, he drew a fine distinction between such misanthropy as sprang from a noble nature and from one that was innately corrupt.

'The misanthropy of a **Timon of Athens** is something quite different from the malevolence of the wicked. That arises from an objective recognition of the wickedness and folly of men in general, it does not fall on individuals, though individuals may give the first impetus ; it concerns all, and each individual is merely looked on as an example. It is even a certain noble displeasure that only arises out of the consciousness of a better nature that has revolted against unexpected wickedness. On the other hand, ordinary malevolence, ill-will and malice are quite subjective, arising not from cognition but from Will, which is constantly crossed by collision with other persons and therefore hates individuals, *i.e.*, all ; yet only partially, separately, and solely from a subjective point of view. He will love some few with whom he is united by relationship, habit or interest, although they are not better than the rest. The misanthrope is related to the merely malevolent, as the ascetic who gives up the will to live, who resigns, to the suicide, who, it is true, takes his own life, but dreads some certain event in life more, so that his fear outweighs his love to live. Malevolence and suicide are only called forth by certain cases ; misanthropy and resignation include the whole of life. Those resemble the ordinary shipper who knows by routine how to sail a certain path on the sea, but is helpless elsewhere ; these are like a skilful navigator who knows the use of compass, chart, quadrant, and chronometer, and so finds his way over the whole world. Malevolence and suicide would disappear if certain circumstances were erased : misanthropy and resignation stand firm and are moved by nothing temporal.'

It may excite surprise why a man who found life so unsatisfactory should care to live. Curiously, however, Schopenhauer was emphatic against suicide. Blind Will had set the puppets of human life in motion, the same power demands their preservation until their natural end. To flee from life is not cowardly but abnormal. It is only the disagreeable present conditions a man desires to quit, he does not deny the will to live ; this may consequently continue after his death and cause him to take shape again in some more unpleasant form. This appears paradoxical, indeed many views held by Schopenhauer were so. He knew this and rather prided himself upon it.

'Whoever is prejudiced by the paradoxicalness of a work, is clearly of opinion that a great deal of wisdom is in circulation, that the world has got very far indeed, and that only details need emendation. But whoever, like Plato, polishes off current opinion with *tois poyyois poyya ookei*, or is convinced with Goethe that the absurd really fills the world, such an one regards the paradoxicalness of any work as a *prima facie*, although by no means a decisive, symptom of its merit.

'It would be a beautiful world in which truth could not be paradox, virtue suffer no pain, and every good thing be certain of approbation.'

Schopenhauer early recognised in what manner his philosophy differed from the common. 'The Philosophasters can never get outside themselves and deliberately regard the world and their inner being ; they think to spin out a system from conceptions : it becomes worthy its origin.

'The subject for philosophy, the art whose mere materials are conceptions, is only idea. Let the philosopher seize the ideas of all such things as exist in consciousness and which appear as objects : he must stand like Adam before a new creation and give each thing its name, he will then strip and starve the dead notions, drawing forth the ever-living idea, like the sculptor his statue from the marble.'

He anticipated the criticisms his work would call forth.

'After every important discovery detractors spring up to point out that the same thing was already spoken of in some old chronicles ; these will find traces of my teaching in nearly all the philosophies of all ages. Not only in the Vedas, in Plato and Kant, the living matter of Bruno, Glisson and Spinoza, the slumbering monads of Leibnitz, but throughout in all philosophies, the oldest and the newest. Yet always in the most varied dress, interwoven with absurdities that strike the eye, in the most grotesque shapes, in which one can only recognise them by careful scrutiny. It appears to me like finding in all animals the type of man, but so strangely mauled and unfinished, sometimes stinted, sometimes monstrous, now a rude attempt and now a caricature. The presumption that dares this comparison is merely a corollary of the presumption that exists in setting up a new philosophic system at all ; for the doing so is an assertion that all previous attempts are failures, and that one's own is a success ; whoever does not think so, and yet thrusts a new system upon the world, is necessarily a charlatan. It has been with philosophy till now as it is in an auction-room, where everyone who speaks last annuls all that has been said before.

'I confess, however, that I do not believe my teaching could ever have arisen before the Upanishads, Plato, and Kant could throw their light combined into men's minds. But truly, as Diderot says, many columns have stood, and the sun shone on them all, yet only Memnon's sang.'

Schopenhauer was never communicative, his works were for the world, his life was his own. Little is therefore known of his outer history during these four years at Dresden, though such ample memoranda remain of his thoughts. It appears he mixed chiefly among literary men with whom he was, strange to say, popular, notwithstanding his withering sarcasms and intellectual haughtiness. The three most popular novelists of the day, Heun, Schulze, and Schilling were the men he saw most constantly, all of them his seniors, excellent companions, witty and amusing. Schilling's eighty volumes of tales were already forgotten in Schopenhauer's old age, a circumstance he regretted, as he valued them for their inexhaustible fund of humour. Neither are the other two remembered, except as names ; their works slumber in oblivion. The poet Ludvig Tieck also lived at Dresden, and for some time Schopenhauer visited much at his house, the central point of literary society. Tieck drew all intellectual men and women around him, and his wonderful dramatic readings and table talk were widely known. Some severe remarks let fall by Schopenhauer against Tieck's intimate friend Frederick Schlegel broke this intimacy The truest friend he made at this time was Johann Gottlieb von Quandt, the art critic, who remained devoted to him till death. Schopenhauer's sarcasms did not spare even his friends, Quandt and he were of accord on many subjects and each derived pleasure from their intercourse, but Quandt would often remind Schopenhauer in after years of how little he had valued his opinion. 'If I ever had at all a good idea,' he said, 'you always asked me where I had read that, as if I picked up all my thoughts out of the dustbins of literature.'

Under such conditions, slowly and steadily was Schopenhauer's opus maximum, 'Die Welt als Wille und Vorstellung,' brought to an end. It contains his entire system, in it he reached the apex of his intellectual life, all his later writings are mere brilliant commentaries and illustrations. In the spring of 1818, the manuscript was sent to Messrs. Brockhaus, of Leipzig, who gladly undertook its publication, paying the author a ducat the printed sheet.

'Whoever has accomplished a great immortal work will be as little hurt by its reception from the public, or swayed by the opinions of critics, as a sane man in a madhouse is affected by the upbraidings and aggressions of the insane.' These were the words Schopenhauer wrote as he sent his great work into the world.

CHAPTER V - HIS 'OPUS MAXIMUM'

WE will now attempt some definition of the leading conception of *Die Welt als Wille und Vorstellung*, the great work on which Schopenhauer rested his reputation. Anything like a full analysis would be beyond our limits, but it may be possible briefly to convey a sufficient idea of its nature and scope, to indicate the writer's place in the history of speculation. His own claim was to be regarded as the immediate successor of Kant, and such, no doubt considered merely as a metaphysician, he was. Philosophically however, he is chiefly interesting as a representative of Indian thought in the west, and a consequent precursor of that fusion of the European spirit of experimental research, with the Eastern genius for abstract speculation, which, fostered by the mutual intercourse of both peoples, is beginning to exert so powerful an influence upon each. Or, to put the matter somewhat differently, he may be described as helping to indicate that transition of the European mind from a monotheistic to a pantheistic view of the universe, which began with Giordano Bruno, and of which the end is not yet.

Every philosophy and religion aiming to give a rational account of the universe must be either mundane or extra-mundane ; it must either regard the cause of the Cosmos as contained in the Cosmos itself, or refer the existence of the latter to the interposition of some external agent. At a certain stage of man's intellectual progress the latter conclusion seems absolutely forced upon him. Having fully mastered the truth that every effect implies a cause, for ordinary common sense is not easily convinced that cause and effect are either unrelated, or, as has been recently maintained, identical, he is irresistibly impelled to seek the cause of every effect which he witnesses. Finding himself surrounded by phenomena inexplicable in the actual state of his knowledge, he naturally ascribes them to a cause external to the universe, and independent of it. The flaming thunderbolt, for instance, seems sufficient evidence of the existence of some agent by whom it is hurled upon the earth. No javelin of wood and iron, the reasoner knows well, could be cast forth without the immediate or mediate agency of an arm, and why a javelin of fire? It requires a considerable intellectual advance, ere he is able to discern that the same degree of evidence does not exist for the fact and for the hypothesis by which it is sought to be explained, that the former is a matter of observation, and the latter of inference. The recognition of this truth signalises the birth of philosophy, which, alike in its speculative and practical aspect, may be defined for our present purpose as the endeavour to substitute knowledge for hypothesis : and the idea of an extraneous agency as the cause of the Universe being necessarily an hypothesis, although a very plausible one, the tendency of philosophical speculation, as such, is necessarily to weaken this notion.

It is perceived in turn, that if the connection of the assumed cause and the effect is necessary, the two are inseparable, and that to deny the inevitableness of their connection is to assert that the supposed extraneous cause of the Universe might conceivably have been unattended by any effect whatever. It obviously follows that if the Universe is not to be explained on the hypothesis of such extraneous agency, it can only be explicable as the result of forces immanent in itself; and as all these forces admit of being comprehended under the general title of Universe, and regarded as modifications of a single existence, the tendency of this course of speculation must be to establish an absolute unity of cause, and a virtual identity of cause and effect the *natura naturans* and *natura naturata* of Spinoza. This mental process is exhibited with great clearness in the gradual transition from the naturalistic polytheism of the primitive Hindoos to Brahminical Pantheism ; and on the experimental side, not less evidently in the history of European science.

The great significance of Schopenhauer arises from his active participation in this characteristic intellectual movement of his age, and from his having at the same time formulated the doctrine of universal unity in a manner practically original and peculiar to himself. His claim could not be better stated than in his own words.

'My age,' he says, 'after the teaching of Bruno, Spinoza, and Schelling, had perfectly understood that all things are but one : but the nature of this unity, and the rationale of its appearance as plurality, were reserved for me to explain.'

The theory thus referred to admits of being very briefly stated. It is fully conveyed by the hardly translatable title of Schopenhauer's principal work: *Die Welt als Wille und Vorstellung*. As all philosophers must, he here makes a distinction between the actual substratum, the real essence of existence, and the merely phenomenal form of its manifestation. Spinoza had called the former *natura naturans*, the latter *natura naturata*, and had elsewhere described phenomena as the *modes* of the one infinite and eternal Substance. Schopenhauer endeavours to define this Substance itself, and declares it to be a Will. From the idea of Will, action is inseparable ; and the existence of the phenomenal world is, according to him, sufficiently explained by regarding it as the result of the craving of the eternal Will, the substratum of all existence, to manifest itself in an external form. This Will, in a word, is a will to live.

So far there is nothing original in Schopenhauer's doctrine, beyond its lively and characteristic method of expression. It is precisely the same as the Buddhist teaching, which refers all existence to desire, and differs but slightly from the religious mysticism which points out that the recognition of Divine attributes implies the necessity of creation, since love and wisdom must be dormant without an object to call them forth.

Schopenhauer's peculiarity however is, that while other thinkers have usually assumed Intelligence as an attribute of Will, Intelligence is to him but a mere phenomenon.

'This resolution,' he says, 'of the so long indivisible Ego or Soul into two heterogeneous constituents, is for philosophy what Lavoisier's resolution of water into oxygen and hydrogen has been for chemistry.'

'The world in itself,' to borrow Mr. Oxenford's condensation of Schopenhauer's principle, 'is one enormous Will, constantly rushing into life.'

Will is the condition of all existence, sentient and insentient. 'Others,' he proudly says, 'have asserted the Will's freedom, I prove its omnipotence.'

We cannot do better than translate M. Ribot's terse and lucid summary of Schopenhauer's teaching on this capital point.

'Since Will is the centre of ourselves and of all things, we must give it the first rank. It is its due, although since Anaxagoras Intelligence has usurped its place. In the volume which completes his great work, Schopenhauer has written an interesting chapter on the "Pre-eminence of the Will," and on the inferiority of the thinking principle considered as a mere "cerebral phenomenon." To speak more exactly, Intelligence is only a *tertiary* phenomenon. The first place belongs to the Will, the second to the organism, which is its immediate objectivation, the third to thought, which is a function of the brain, and consequently of the organism. Therefore one may say Intelligence is the secondary phenomenon, the organisation the primary phenomenon ; the Will is metaphysical, the Intelligence is physical ; the Intelligence is the semblance, the Will the thing in itself; and in a still more metaphorical sense : Will is the substance of the man, Intelligence the accident ; Will is the matter, Intelligence the form ; Will is the heat, Intelligence the light.'

This is shown by the following facts :

'1. All knowledge presupposes a subject and an object, but the object is the primitive and essential element, it is the prototype whose ectype is the subject. If we examine our knowledge we shall see that what is most generally known in us is the Will with its affections : to strive, to desire, to fly, to hope, to fear, to love, to hate ; in a word, all that relates to our well or ill-being, all that is a modification of willing or not willing. Therefore even in our Will is the primitive and essential element.

'2. The basis of consciousness in every animal is *desire*. This fundamental fact is shown by the tendency to preserve life and well-being, and to reproduce. It is this tendency which, according as it is thwarted or gratified, produces joy, anger, fear, hatred, love, selfishness, &c. This fundament is common to the polypus and to man. The difference between animals springs from a difference in understanding. Therefore Will is the primitive and essential, Intelligence the secondary and accidental fact.

'3. If we examine the animal series we shall see that as we descend Intelligence becomes feebler and more imperfect, while the Will undergoes no similar degradation. In the smallest insect the Will is entire, it wills what it wills quite as completely as man. Will is always identical with itself, its function is of the very simplest kind ; to will, or not to will.

'4. Intelligence tires ; Will is indefatigable. Intelligence being secondary and physical, is, as such, subject to the *force of inertia*, which explains why intellectual work requires moments of repose, and why age causes degeneracy of the brain, followed by imbecility or insanity. When we see men like Swift, Kant, Walter Scott, Southey, Wordsworth, and so many others sink into childishness, or into a state of intellectual feebleness, how can we deny that Intelligence is a pure organ, a function of the body, while the body is a function of the Will?

'5. Intelligence plays its secondary part so well that it can only adequately accomplish its function while the Will is silent and does not interpose ; it has long been remarked that "passion is the declared enemy of prudence." Bacon justly says :

"'The eye of the human understanding is not a naked organ of perception (*lumen siccum*), but an eye imbued with moisture by Will and Passion. Man always believes what he determines to believe."

'6. The functions of Intelligence, on the contrary, are augmented by the stimulation of the Will, when both act in concert. This is another common remark, that " Necessity is mother of the arts." "*Facit indignatio versum*" &c. Even in animals, facts quoted by those who have observed them, show that when Will commands, Intelligence obeys. But the converse is not true. Intelligence is eclipsed by Will, as the moon by the sun.

'7. If Will took its origin from Intelligence, as is generally admitted, there ought to be much will where there is much knowledge and reason. But it is not always thus, as the experience of all ages exemplifies. Intelligence is the instrument of Will, as the hammer is that of the smith.

'8. Let us consider on the one hand the virtues and faults of Intelligence, on the other those of Will ; history and experience teach that they are entirely independent of each other. Among examples which crowd upon us, 'we will mention only one, Francis Bacon. Intellectual gifts have always been held as presents from Nature or the gods. Moral virtues are considered as innate, as really interior and personal. Thus all religions have promised eternal rewards, not to the virtues of the mind, which are exterior and accidental, but to the virtues of character, which are the man himself. And lasting friendships are far oftener those whose foundation rests on an accord of Will, than those whose foundation is an analogy of Intelligence. Hence the power possessed by the spirit of party, sect, faction, &c.

'9. We should also remember the difference that every one makes between the *heart* and the *head*. The heart, the *primum mobile* of animal life, is rightly used as synonymous with the Will. We say *heart* whenever there is Will, *head* whenever there is Knowledge. We embalm the hearts of heroes, not their brains ; we preserve the skull of a poet, a philosopher.

'10. On what does the identity of personality rest? Not on the matter of the body, which changes in a few years ; nor on the form, which changes entirely and in all its parts ; nor on the consciousness, for that rests on memory ; age and maladies, physical and mental, destroy it. It can therefore only rest on the identity of the Will and the immortality of character. "Man is incarnate in the heart, not in the head."

'11. The Will to live, with the consequent horror of death that results, is a fact anterior to, and independent of, all intelligence.

'12. The secondary and dependent nature of Intelligence is plainly shown by its character of intermittence and periodicity. In profound sleep all consciousness ceases. Only the centre of our being, the metaphysical principle, the *primum mobile*, does not stop, or life would cease. While the brain rests, and with it the intelligence, the organic functions continue their work. The brain, whose proper office is to know, is a sentinel placed in the head by Will, to guard the outer world through the window of the senses ; hence its condition of constant effort and continual tension, and hence the necessity of relieving it at its post.'—Th. Ribot, 'La Philosophic de Schopenhauer,' pp. 69-72.

Schopenhauer's philosophy is therefore a phase of Pantheism, a modification of the system represented in Europe by Bruno[3], Spinoza, and Schelling, though differentiated from their philosophies by a bisection of the Soul, Ego, or First Principle, into two factors described as Will and Intelligence, a separation capable, according to himself, of resolving the contradictions charged against Pantheism in general. If we first inquire into the genesis of this theory, which did not of course come spontaneously into being without intellectual antecedents, we shall probably find that it may be defined with equal propriety as an engrafting of Indian Pantheism upon Kant, or *vice versa*. Schopenhauer himself magnanimously pointed out that he had been in some degree anticipated by the Wolfian philosopher Crusius, to whom he applied the humorous imprecation, *Pereant qui ante nos nostra dixere*. Kant, his first master, had taught him the illusiveness of space and time, and the unreality of the world of phenomena. In the Upanishads, the Vedanta philosophy, and such other documents of Indian wisdom as were accessible to the European world in his youth, of which his early note-books show him to have been an enthusiastic student, he found the same ideas reiterated in a mystical form congenial to his imagination and combined with that pessimistic view of life co-nate with his hypochondriacal temperament. The peculiar stress he was led to place upon the Will as the real cause of existence may be logically defensible, but was no doubt in the first instance subjective, the reflection of his own individuality. 'An enormous Will, constantly rushing into life,' would be no bad description of his own spiritual constitution. He must also throughout his life have been painfully conscious of the discordance of his philosophical principles with his habitual practice.

'I preach sanctity,' he said, 'but I am myself no saint.'

The Will, the blind instinctive impulse, was with him continually getting the upper hand of the regulating faculty, the Reason. It was natural therefore, that he should regard the former as the primary substance, the latter as the accident or phenomenon.!

'Intelligence,' as his teaching is condensed by M. Ribot, 'has but one end, the conservation of the individual. All else is ornament and superfluity.'

This being so, the Will recognised by Schopenhauer as the basis of Being must be a Will to Live, and the question immediately arises whether this Will be a good one or a bad one. Schopenhauer's answer is apparent from what we have already told in his biography. He holds with the Indian and Singhalese schools of Buddhism (northern Buddhism seems to teach otherwise) that desire is the root of all evil, and that all desire may be reduced to the affirmation (Bejahung) of the Will to Live. By suppressing desire we suppress evil, but we suppress existence also. The whole world therefore 'lieth in wickedness;' it is a world that ought never to have been. The ethical and practical bearings of this conception will be better discussed elsewhere. We may remark here, however, upon the practical disadvantages under which Schopenhauer is placed in comparison with Spinoza, by the primary importance he assigns to Will, and his divorce between volition and intelligence. No foundation is thus left for his universe but a blind unintelligent force, which could not reasonably be an object of reverence, even were its operation as beneficial as, according to Schopenhauer, it is the reverse. No religion consequently remains, except that of simple philanthropy and self-denial. To Spinoza, on the contrary, Will and Intelligence alike, along with the entire material and spiritual universe, are but the manifestations of an infinite Substance, which, as infinite, must necessarily be manifested in an infinity of ways utterly beyond our comprehension. To Schopenhauer the universe has a centre, and that centre is a mere blind impulse. To Spinoza, as has been finely said, the centre is everywhere and the circumference nowhere. The one, therefore, fully provides for the religious reverence the other abolishes. At the same time it must be added that the acceptance of Schopenhauer's view of the Will as the ultimate cause, and the denial of all qualities to it beyond instinctive impulse, by no means bind the disciple to the acceptance of his pessimistic view of the universe. As Schopenhauer himself admits, the appreciation of phenomena varies greatly as the interpreter is by temperament εὔκολος or δύσκολος. Schopenhauer's disciple may be as enchanted with the beauty, harmony, and convenience of the world as his master is impressed with its misery and wretchedness ; yet, if accepting his postulate of Will as the prime factor of Being, he is still speculatively his disciple. Very few of Schopenhauer's followers have consistently adopted his pessimism. Eduard von Hartmann, a writer of singular power and genius, who gave Schopenhauer's views a great development in his *Philosophic des Unbewussten*, in his last publication betrays a wish to recede from the advanced views he at one time held upon the subject.

It need hardly be added that, although Schopenhauer's cardinal principle is the omnipotence of Will, the freedom of the individual will is strenuously denied by him. All phenomena being but manifestations of the one primary force, are necessarily conditioned by it. No man can change his character, for the character is the Will itself exhibited in a phenomenal form.

'The absolute Will,' says Mr. Oxenford, interpreting him, 'which lay beyond the jurisdiction of causality, has forced itself into the world of phenomena in an individual shape, and it must take the consequences, that is to say, a subjugation to that law of cause and effect by which the whole world of phenomena is governed. The character, which is the Idea of the human individual, just as gravitation is one of the Ideas of matter, is born with him, and cannot be altered. The knowledge of the individual may be enlarged, and consequently may be put in a better track, by learning that his natural desires will be more gratified if he obeys the laws of society than if he rises against them ; but the character remains the same.'

This admission however seems to involve a larger concession to Intelligence than is quite consistent with the spirit of Schopenhauer's philosophy. His theory too, while thoroughly necessarian as respects the irresistible influence of motive upon action, is opposed to necessarianism, in the less refined and more popular aspect presented in the common phrase 'Man is the creature of circumstances.' He must have concurred with Mr. Mill ('Autobiography,' p. 169), that though our character is formed by circumstances, our desires can do much to shape those circumstances,' and that, 'our will, by influencing some of our circumstances, can modify our future habits or capabilities' of willing.'

A better opportunity will occur of discussing Schopenhauer's relation to such practical problems as the above. For the present it must suffice to say that he was by no means indifferent to them, that in fact the kernel of his philosophy consists in its practical application. It would be an utter error to conclude that because, in common with almost all other metaphysicians, he held the world of sensuous perceptions to be phenomenal and illusive, he was therefore a mere trifler with empty abstractions, or a propounder of dialectical juggles. On the contrary, he is the most concrete of writers and thinkers, invariably resorts when possible to some illustration derived from visible or tangible objects, and is never weary of ridiculing and denouncing those philosophers who deal solely in abstractions.

'All thought at first hand' he says, 'is performed by means of images of sensible objects. Writing and discourse themselves strive to convey to another's mind the same distinct realisation of an object which the writer or operator has, or should have, before his own. If they fail to achieve this, they are naught. A book can at best only impart truth at second-hand.'

In this spirit lie laid the greatest stress upon scientific research, as bringing the student into immediate contact with concrete reality. He especially venerated Bichat, who had, he considered, already expressed his own great principle of the duality of the Will and the intelligence under a physiological form ; the anatomist's 'organic life' being the physiological equivalent of Schopenhauer's ' Will,' and his 'animal life' of the latter's 'Intelligence.'

It is interesting to speculate what reception he would have given to the great scientific discoveries and theories which have since his time so profoundly modified the course of European thought. He died in the year of the discovery of the spectroscope. One of the last things he read was a review of 'The Origin of Species' in the *Times*, and, as Dr. Asher points out, he had to a certain extent anticipated the generalisation of the universal 'struggle for existence,' with its corollary of 'the survival of the fittest,' a conclusion perfectly in harmony with his own conception of the absolute Will perpetually bursting into life. But he does not appear to have attained to the recognition of this conflict as a factor in the gradual evolution of species. This evolution he admitted, but his account of the process was singularly lame: a serpent, for instance, might have laid lizard's eggs 'in a happy hour,' the lizards would propagate the new type until the occurrence of a similar interruption of continuity, and so on. This was an equivalent to an acknowledgment that he could give no rational account of the matter. He was probably tempted to make light of physiological difficulties by his deep perception of the substantial identity of the moral and intellectual nature in man and animals, on which he is never tired of enlarging. The other great scientific generalisation of our time, the theory of accumulated hereditary impressions by which Mr. Spencer has virtually settled the controversy between the champions of experience and intuition, would probably have been eagerly welcomed by him. He insisted much, on heredity, and had a theory of his own that the male parent represents the primal Will, the female the functional Intelligence, which, however, seems to rest on no more solid basis than his preference for his father over his mother.

To sum up, Schopenhauer is a powerful though eccentric representative of the general tendency of philosophic minds to find rest in the conception of the Universe as Unity. He has not, as he flattered himself, supplied the metaphysical demonstration of this doctrine, and his alleged great discovery is at best a dubious one. But he has devised an original formula which will often be found convenient, has vivified every subject he has touched, and has rendered philosophy the inestimable service of recalling her to concrete realities from barren dialectic. His reverence for the manifestations of Nature as absolute truth, and the study of them as the sole real source of Knowledge, shines forth from every page of his writings. If he misconceived the character and purposes of Nature, it must be owned that she had denied him the especial faculties requisite for the recognition of her grandeur and benevolence. There is something plausible in his pessimism until we consider on how exceedingly contracted and partial, and consequently deceptive view of the universe it is based. Schopenhauer, though so merciless to the foibles of philosophers, was not exempt from the nearly universal one of assuming that all the facts of existence can be comprehended in a formula with as much accuracy as the composition of water can be expressed by chemical notation.

His philosophy may in one aspect be viewed as a sublime example of the cardinal proposition of speculative thought, the ideality and unreality of apparent existence, the utter dependence of the preconceived object, be it in appearance never so substantial and majestic, upon the perceiving subject. Such a system, elaborated with however rigid logic, fails to commend itself to the instincts of a world of beings diverse in mental constitution from its author. For mankind in the mass it remains an idle play of ingenuity, or an empty abstraction. Such exercises of the reason, however, have ere this paved the way for faith ; they have shown themselves the precursors, if not the actual parents of mighty religions, commending themselves to the needs and instincts of humanity at large, and in this manner wielding the influence denied to them in their character of philosophical speculations. Schopenhauer may yet prove the Kapila of a new Buddha.

CHAPTER VI - HIS SOJOURN IN ITALY

ON the completion of his work, Schopenhauer did not resolve himself into Nirvana, as might perhaps have been reasonably expected; on the contrary, without even waiting for proof sheets, he set off at once to the brightest and most optimistic land under the sun, the very land of promise, 'the land of lands,' fair Italy. It has been well said, that the habit of looking at the night side of life vanishes and appears unnatural amid the passionate glowing nature of a southern sky. An unkind environment often breeds a false pessimism ; but that must be genuine which can arise or survive in genial surroundings. That Schopenhauer retained his pessimism in Italy is a convincing proof, were further needed, of its unaffected sincerity. It was comprehensible enough in the hard cold north, but to hold it in a land where everything smiles, where Nature herself invites us to take existence easily and let care go hang, where the very air breathes light-heartedness, where *dolce far niente* is the life motto of the natives, is another matter. The chronicles of this Italian journey are all but a blank. Schopenhauer grew more and more reserved as the years went on, and there are neither journals nor letters to supply the gap. Furthermore, it was his own express desire ; he shunned publicity. ' I will not have my private life given over to the cold and malevolent curiosity of the public,' was his reply many years later, when pressed to give more details than he had furnished to the biographical dictionaries. His notebooks supplied the place of a journal ; but as they deal rather with the reflections suggested by events, than with events themselves, they do not throw much light on the incidents of his journey.

Schopenhauer crossed the barrier Alps, in the proud consciousness of having written a great work for mankind ; he waited to see the result. He was not quite so indifferent as to its reception, as he would make believe. The Fourfold Root had been well received by the critics, and had called forth more attention than is usual with formal academical exercises; he was justified in expecting that this larger work would at least command the same regard. He corrected the proof sheets that were sent after him, and looked forward to the publication. His feelings found vent in verse.

Unverschdmte Verse.

Aus langgehegten, tiefgefiihlten Schmerzen

Wand sich's empor axis meinem innern Herzen ;

Es festzuhalten hab' ich lang gerungen,

Doch weiss ich, dasz zuletzt es mir gelungen.

Mogt Euch drum immer wie Ihr wollt, gebarden,

Des Werkes Leben konnt Ihr nicht gefahrden ;

Aufhalten konnt Ihr's, nimmermehr vernichten,

Ein Denkmal \vird die Nachwelt mir errichten.

Meanwhile, be visited the principal towns in North Italy ; frequenting the art galleries and the theatre, and studying Italian, in which he was already proficient. It was in Italy that he conceived his fondness for Rossini's music ; he would go repeatedly to hear his operas. Of the Italian authors, his favourite was, strangely enough, Petrarch, that singer of Laura and love.

'Of all Italian writers, I prefer my much loved **Petrarch**. No poet in the whole world has ever surpassed him in depth and fervency of feeling, and its expression which goes straight to the heart. Therefore, I much prefer his sonnets, Trionfi and Canzoni, to the phantastic follies of **Ariosto** and horrid distortions of **Dante**. I find the natural flow of words which comes straight from the heart much more congenial than Dante's studied, even affected chariness of speech. He has always been, and will remain the poet of my heart. I am only strengthened in my opinion by the most perfect "present time" that dares to speak disdainfully of Petrarch. A sufficient proof would be the comparison of Dante and Petrarch in their house attire, *i.e.*, in prose, if we placed together the beautiful books of Petrarch, rich in thought and truth, "De Vita Solitaria," "De Contempta Munrli," "Consolatio utriusque Fortunse," &c., with the fruitless dreary scholasticism of Dante.'

Dante's didactic manner was not to his taste ; he considered the whole Inferno as an apotheosis of cruelty, and the last Canto but one, a glorification of want of honour and conscience. Neither did he affect Ariosto or Boccaccio, indeed he frequently expressed his perplexity at the latter's 'European fame;' seeing he narrated only *chroniques scandaleuses*. Alfieri and Tasso he liked, but as secondary lights merely : he did not think Tasso worthy to be ranked as fourth with the three great poets of Italy.

In artistic matters he was, on the whole, more attracted to sculpture and architecture than to painting.

This would not be curious and out of harmony with the general character of his mind, had not his intimacy with Goethe involved him in the study of colour.

Schopenhauer would never allow that these two years of Italian travel had been happy; he contended that while others journeyed for pleasure, he did so to gather materials for his system, and he transcribed Aristotle's axiom : ὁ φρόνιμος τὸ ἄλυπον διώκει, οὐ τὸ ἡδύ, into his note book. Still he always recalled these years with peculiar pleasure, as far as he would admit pleasure in anything. To the last days of his life, he could not mention Venice without a tremour in his voice, which revealed that the love that held him entranced there was not wholly forgotten, if dead. Surely, this note written in Bologna, the 19th of November, 1818,. betrays some contentment ?

'Just because all happiness is negative, it happens that when at last we are in a condition of well-being, we are totally unaware of it, and allow everything to pass easily and softly before us, until the state is over. Only the loss, which makes itself positively felt, brings into relief the vanished happiness ; only then we notice what we have neglected to secure, and remorse associates itself to privation.'

Schopenhauer's longest stay was made in Venice. Byron was there at the time, also chained to the enchanted city by female charms. It is strange they never met. Schopenhauer had the greatest admiration for Byron's genius, and mentally they would have agreed. Neither did he encounter Shelley, nor Leopardi. A dialogue after the manner of Leopardi, in which he and the young Count were confronted, was published in the 'Eivista Contemporanea,' of 1858, and Schopenhauer could not rest till he had secured a copy. It gave him keen delight on account of his association with the young man whom he so greatly admired (and to whom by the way he thought the writer, De Sanctis, had not rendered justice) and also because it proved that his philosophy had penetrated into Italy.

He was not often content with writings about his works ; lie never considered himself to have been read with sufficient care, but this man, he said, had absorbed him *in succum et sanguinem*.

Schopenhauer wrote at Venice on his first arrival : 'Whoever is suddenly transported into a totally strange country or town, where reigns a very different mode of life and even speech from that to which he is accustomed, feels like a person who has stepped into cold water. He is suddenly touched by a temperature widely different from his own, he feels a powerful deliberate influence acting from without, which distresses him ; he is in a strange element in which he cannot move with ease. Added to that, he fears that because everything attracts his notice, he also is attracting the notice of everybody. As soon as he is calmed and has accustomed himself to his surroundings, and has absorbed some of their temperature, he feels as remarkably at ease as the man does in the cold water. He has assimilated himself to the element, and therefore, having ceased to occupy himself with his person, turns his attention solely to his environment; to which, just because of this objective neutral contemplation, he feels himself superior, instead of being oppressed by it, as before.'

'In travelling where novelties of all kinds press in upon us, mental food is often supplied so rapidly from without that there is no time for digestion. We regret that the quickly shifting impressions can leave no permanent imprint. In reality, however, it is with this as it is with reading. How often we regret not being able to retain in the memory one-thousandth part of what is read ! It is comforting in both cases to know that the seen as well as the read has made a mental impression before it is forgotten, and thus forms the mind and nourishes it, while that which is retained in the memory merely fills and swells the hollow of the head with matter which remains ever foreign to it, because it has not been absorbed, and therefore the recipient can be as empty as before.'

Schopenhauer held that in travelling we recognise how rooted is public and national opinion, and how hard it is to change a people's mode of thought.

'When we shun one misfortune, we run to meet another ; when we fly from the national thoughts of one country, we find the different but equally bad ones of another. May Heaven deliver us from this vale of misery.'

'In travelling we see human life in many perceptibly different forms, and it is this which makes travelling so interesting. But in doing so we only see the outer side of human life ; that is, not more than is always accessible to strangers and universally evident. On the other hand, we never see the people's inner life, its heart and centre, where the real action takes place and character manifests itself. .... Therefore in travelling we see the world like a painted landscape, with a wide horizon embracing many things, but without any foreground. It is this which induces weariness of travel.'

He thoughtfully studied the Italians, their ways and their religion. Of the latter he says :

'The Catholic religion is an order to obtain heaven by begging, because it would be too troublesome to earn it. The priests are the brokers for this transaction.'

'All positive religion is after all a usurper of the throne which belongs by right to philosophy ; philosophers will therefore always oppose it, even if they should regard it as a necessary evil, a crutch for the sickly weakness of most minds.'

'Naked truth is powerless to restrain coarse natures and keep them from wrong and cruelty, because they cannot grasp it. Hence the need of fallacies, stories, parables, and positive doctrines.'

In December (1818), 'Die Welt als Wille und Vorstellung' first saw the light. Schopenhauer sent a copy to Goethe. After he removed to Naples in the spring of 1819, Goethe acknowledged the gift through Adele Schopenhauer, a special favourite of the old poet's.

'Goethe received your book with great pleasure,' writes Adele, 'immediately cut up the whole thick work into two parts and then began to read it. An hour after he sent me the enclosed scrap with the message that he thanked you much and thought the whole book was good, because he had always the good fortune to open books at the most remarkable places ; thus he had read with great pleasure the pages he mentions [4], and he hopes soon to write his real opinions more fully to you, but until then he wishes me to tell you this. A few days after Ottilie told me that the father was sitting over the book, perusing it with an eagerness she had never before observed. He told her that he had now a pleasure in store for the whole year, because he was going to read it from beginning to end, and thought it would require quite that time. He said to me that it was quite a great happiness to him that you were still so attached to him, notwithstanding your disagreement about the theory of colours, in which your way diverged from his. He said that in your book he was especially pleased by the clearness of representation and diction, although your language differs from that of others, and one must accustom oneself to name things as you desire. But when this advantage has once been gained, and he knew that horse was not to be called horse, but cavallo, and Grod, Dio or otherwise, then he could read comfortably and easily. The whole arrangement pleased him also ; only the unwieldy size left him no peace, and so he persuaded himself that the work consisted of two volumes. I hope soon to see him again alone and perhaps he may say something more satisfactory. At any rate you are the only author whom Goethe reads in this manner and so seriously.'

Nevertheless Schopenhauer remained of opinion that Goethe did not read him with sufficient attention ; the poet had outlived his slender interest in philosophy.

At Naples Schopenhauer chiefly associated with young Englishmen. The English had through life a special attraction for him ; he thought them to have come near to being the greatest people in the world, that only certain prejudices hindered them from actually being so. His knowledge of the language and his accent were so perfect that even Englishmen would for some time mistake him for a countryman, an error that always elated him.

All he saw served to confirm or elaborate his philosophical theories. A picture by a young Venetian artist, Ajes, exhibited at Capo di Monte, especially struck him, as endorsing his theory with regard to tears, namely, that they spring from self-pity. The subject represented the scene from the Odyssey when Ulysses weeps at the court of King Alcinous, the Phaeacian, on hearing his own woes sung, 'This is the highest expression of self-pity.'

Schopenhauer had now attained to the full maturity of power and life. According to him the genius of men only lasts as long as the beauty of women, namely fifteen years, from the twentieth to at most the thirty-fifth year. 'The twenties and the young thirties are for the intellect what May is for the trees, during which season only they put forth buds whose later development is the fruit.' In personal appearance he must have been remarkable, but his beauty was of the soul, not of the face ; his eyes flashed fire even in his old age, and in youth their keen, clear blue lighted up his massive head. It was about this time that an old gentleman, a perfect stranger, addressed him in the street, saying he would be a great man some day. An Italian, also a stranger, came up and said : 'Signore, lei deve avere fatto qualche grande opera : non so cosa sia, ma lo vedo al suo viso.' A Frenchman, who sat opposite to him at a table-d'hote, suddenly exclaimed : 'Je voudrais savoir ce qu'il pense de nous autres, nous devons paraitre bien petits a ses yeux;' and a young Englishman flatly refused all entreaties to take another place, with : 'No, I'll sit here ; I like to see his intellectual face.'

In repose he resembled Beethoven; both had the same square head, but Schopenhauer's must have been larger, as is proved by a cast taken after death, which shows its unusual size. The width between the eyes was remarkable ; he could wear no ordinary spectacles. His height was medium, his figure square, muscular, and slight, his shoulders broad, his fine head was carried on a throat too short for beauty. Curly fair hair fell on his shoulders and forehead ; as a youth a fair moustache covered his well-formed mouth, which in old age fell in and lengthened as he lost his teeth. His nose was of singular beauty, and so were his small hands. He himself drew a sharp distinction between a man's intellectual and moral physiognomy ; those he sought in the eye and forehead, these in the mouth and chin. He was satisfied with the former in himself, but not at all with the latter. In his dress he was scrupulously neat and elegant, his carriage was aristocratic and slightly haughty. He always wore a tailcoat, white cravat, and shoes, and had his coats copied from the same pattern, regardless of any change in the fashions. Yet he never appeared remarkable, so completely had he subjugated his dress to his person ; and if people looked after him in the street, as they often did, it was his mien of fire and genius that attracted them, not his attire. Later he was photographed and painted ; of his appearance in manhood there remains only tradition.

In the biography of the laborious antiquary and historian, J. F. Bohmer, is preserved the only mention of Schopenhauer's Roman sojourn. Those were the days of mysticism in German art and religion, which called forth a Bunsen in history; Cornelius and Overbeck in art. The young German artists employed by their Consul to decorate his villa on the Monte Pincio, together with certain poets and journalists, were in the habit of meeting daily at the Cafe Greco, which had become the common centre for Germans in Rome. The poet Rückert, the novelist-poet L. Schefer, optimists by profession, were there about the same time ; indeed many of the most eminent contemporary Germans were gathered together in the Eternal City. Schopenhauer frequented the Cafe Greco like the rest, but it appears that his Mephistophilean wit created a disturbing element among the habitues, which made them wish him away. One day he announced to the assembly that the German nation was the stupidest of all, yet it was so far superior to the rest as to have attained to the point of dispensing with religion. This remark called forth a storm of dismay, and several voices cried : 'Turn the fellow out! Let us throw him out! Out with him!' From that day the philosopher avoided the Cafe Greco, but his views on the Germans remained unchanged. 'The German Fatherland has reared no patriot in me,' he once said ; and he often repeated both to his own countrymen and to French and English, that he was ashamed to be a German, they were so stupid a people. 'If I thought so of my nation,' said a Frenchman in reply, 'I should at least hold my tongue about it.' 'This Schopenhauer is an intolerable wiseacre' (*Narr*), writes Bohmer ; 'for the weal of the community the whole crew of these religionless and un-german philosophers ought to be shut up.'

Schopenhauer led no saintly ascetic life, nor did he pretend to this eminence. He despised women ; he regarded sexual love as one of the most characteristic manifestations of Will, but he was not licentious. He sighed with Byron : 'The more I see of men the less I like them; if I could but say so of women too, all would be well.' He was only different to ordinary men in that he spoke of what others suppress, and his over-zealous disciples who saw the godlike in all his acts, even dragged these to the light of day, and have consequently drawn upon him an imputation he never deserved. Schopenhauer's views coincided with Buddha's utterance that 'There is no passion comparable in power to the sexual passion, there is none other worth mentioning beside it ; were there but one such another, then should no flesh sea salvation!' Hence it was, no doubt, that Schopenhauer feared he could not attain to Nirvana, as he regretfully observed to Dr. Gwinner.

In the midst of this careless dallying among beauty,, he was startled by the news that the Danzig merchant firm, in which a great part of his own and all his mother's fortune was invested, was threatened with bankruptcy. Without delay he started back to Germany. Loss of fortune was of all ills that most dreaded by Schopenhauer, and the one which he felt his peculiar temperament least adapted to endure. He was not fitted for a bread-winner ; his intellect was not of the kind that can be let out for hire; in his inherited independence he always beheld the greatest blessing of his life, since it permitted him the unbroken leisure demanded by his studies.

He writes in the 'Parerga,' under the heading 'Von dem was Einer hat' :

'I do not deem it in any way unworthy of my pen to urge the care of earned and inherited fortune. For to possess at the outset so much that it were possible to live, though alone and without family, comfortably in real independence that is, without working is an in- estimable advantage ; for it is the exemption and immunity from the privation and worry attendant on human life, and thus the emancipation from the universal villanage, the natural lot of mortals. He only who is thus favoured by fate is born a real free man ; for thus only he is *sui juris*, master of his time and his powers, and may say every morning "The day is mine." For this reason, the difference between a man who has a thousand, and one who has a hundred thousand thalers income, is much less than between the former and one who has nothing. Hereditary fortune attains its highest value when it has fallen to the lot of a man, who, endowed with intellectual capacities of a high order, follows pursuits which are incompatible with bread-winning. He is doubly endowed by fate, and can live for his genius, but he will repay his debt to mankind an hundred- fold, for he effects what no other can, and produces something for the good, even for the honour of the community. Another man in this privileged situation will earn the thanks of humanity by philanthropic endeavours. On the other hand he who does not, in some degree at least, try to effect any such thing, who does not by even the thorough acquisition of some science qualify himself to aid mankind, such an one, with an hereditary fortune, is despicable, and a mere idler.'

. . . .

'Now this is reserved for the highest intellectual eminence which we are accustomed to call genius, for genius alone takes as its theme the existence and nature of things in an absolute whole, and then endeavours to express its deep perception of these, according to individual bent, by art, poetry, or philosophy. Therefore for such a nature undisturbed communion with itself, with its thoughts and works, is an urgent need. Solitude is welcome, and leisure is its greatest good. All else may be dispensed with, is at times even a burden. Of such a man only can we say that his centre of gravity falls entirely in himself. Thus it becomes clear, why these very rare persons, even with the best characters, do not show that fervent and boundless sympathy with friends, family, and the common weal, of which many others are capable ; for after all they can console themselves for everything, so long as they have themselves. There is an isolating element in them, which is the more active because others are not entirely sufficient to them, they cannot quite regard them as their equals ; and as they begin to feel everything heterogeneous to them, they accustom themselves to go about among men as different beings, and in their thoughts to apply to them the third and not the first person plural.' . . .

'A man thus inwardly rich, requires nothing from outside except a negative gift, that of free leisure to improve and develop his intellectual capacities, and to enjoy his inner riches, which means the permission every day and every hour, his whole life through, to be entirely himself. When a man is destined to impress, the mark of his intellect upon the whole human race, he can only know one joy or grief, that of seeing his capacities completely developed and being able to accomplish his work, or being hindered in it. Everything else is insignificant ; true to this, we find that in all ages the greatest minds have set the highest value upon leisure, and each man's leisure is worth as much as he himself is worth.'

Shenstone's maxim : 'Liberty is a more invigorating cordial than Tokay,' was a favourite quotation of Schopenhauer's. Filled with the gloomiest forebodings, he hastened to Germany. By his energy and mistrustfulness of fair professions, he was able to secure the bulk of his own fortune. His mother would not listen to advice, and when the final crash came, she and Adele were left almost penniless.

This incident demonstrates that Schopenhauer was no gauche unpractical philosopher ; he would never have fallen into the pit while regarding the stars. With genius he combined common sense, a rare combination which he traced to his merchant father. It is this very quality that makes Schopenhauer, quite apart from his pessimism, so pre-eminently the philosopher for every-day necessities. He had lived in the world, he was no closet theoriser, he knew the world's requirements, needs, demands, his aphorisms and axioms are not too high flown for practice. They are besides, couched in plain, intelligible language, and often express the dim perceptions of every thinking mind.

Though man a thinking being is defined,

Few use the great prerogative of mind ;

How few think justly of the thinking few ;

How many never think, who think they do.

Their number, alas, is legion! and for these neither philosopher, poet, sage, or artist, is needed ; they have a sufficient guide through life in their animal instincts.

CHAPTER VII - HIS DISSATISFIED YEARS

THOUGH the actual loss of fortune sustained by Schopenhauer was insignificant, the event had given his assurance of secured subsistence a shock, which, combined with his innate dread of possible evil, powerfully affected his mind. To save himself from any more dire catastrophe he decided to seek some career. It was natural that should turn to teaching, in which his love for theorising would find full vent. Still he had no notion of making philosophy a means of obtaining a livelihood.

'To model philosophy according to the wishes of the powers that be, and make it the instrument of their plans, so as to obtain money and appointments, seems to me as if a person should receive the sacrament to satisfy his hunger and thirst.'

(This was an oblique stroke at Hegel.)

After some deliberation, he chose Berlin as the city in which he would begin his new mode of life, and moved thither in the spring of 1820. Here, in the intellectual capital of Prussia, among an older and riper class of students, he hoped to find congenial listeners. He confidently expected that his popular style of delivery and the renown of his work : 'Die Welt als Wille und Vorstellung,' would smooth preliminary difficulties, and that before long he would be called to fill an academic chair. He had not expected an instantaneous, overwhelming success for 'Die Welt als Wille und Vorstellung,' such a success would have made him doubt the value of his work, but he had not anticipated that it would meet with less attention than the 'Fourfold Root.' Yet such was the case. Only a few voices made themselves heard concerning it ; these, however, were favourable. Jean Paul wrote of it in his poetic mystic language :

'A bold philosophic many-sided work, full of genius, profoundness, and penetration, but with a depth often hopeless and bottomless, akin to the melancholy sunless lake in Norway, that is barred by a stern rampart of beetling crags, in whose depth only the starry day is reflected, whose surface no bird skims, no wave upheaves.'

Two years Schopenhauer spent in Berlin, in vain efforts to attract an audience. He hated the place and its moral and physical atmosphere. 'One lives there as in a ship at sea ; everything is scarce, expensive, and difficult to procure, the eatables dry and meagre, while the knaveries and deceits of every kind are worse than in the land where the pale citron grows. They not only necessitate the most wearisome caution, but cause those who do not know us to suspect us of all manner of things of which we have never dreamed.' Its society was equally distasteful : the slipshod habits and the pedantry of his philosophical brethren repelled him ; only in the company of well-bred gentlemen and aristocrats did he feel at ease ; and even these found him less approachable as time wore on, and ill success added bitterness to his overflowing stock of contempt for his fellow-men.

Many circumstances combined to render his lectures unpopular. Hegel and Schleiermacher were at the acme of their celebrity, delivering doctrines diametrically opposed to those of Schopenhauer, and more in conformity with the feeble energies of an age disgusted with a war, begun in enthusiasm, ended in despondence, that left the nation in a political condition of unrest and chaos. A mild sophistry better suited their requirements than Schopenhauer's root and branch exterminating doctrines. Feeling himself ahead of his generation, he lectured, as he wrote, from the height at which he had arrived ; forgetting that his audience was not there by a long way, and that he must lead them gently up the intermediate steep, if they were to attain his altitude; that ordinary minds could not achieve the *salto mortale* of genius. To have been popular, and therefore useful, he should have condescended to study the spirit of his time, a very definitely emphasised spirit, contemptible and small though it was, and then, with this knowledge, spoken to its understanding, and led it by degrees to the perception of exalted truths. By such means, by acting from within, he could have imperceptibly expanded and elevated the current thought. He could not stoop so low, this haughty mind, whose genius was not of the order that can accommodate itself to stoop. He wanted to remodel, renovate from without, wanted to act in the world of intellect in the very revolutionary manner he most detested in the sphere of politics. What wonder that he failed! Public opinion, stupid as it is, is never without a very sound substratum of common sense, that resents mistakes, though it fails to recognise with precision from what causes these errors have sprung. Schopenhauer cannot be said to have been wholly wanting in perception of this fact: still he tried to run his head through a wall, and the wall was too hard for him. Added to this he was utterly careless of others' feelings. What wonder once more that he failed, when we read how he began his initiatory lecture.

'Soon after Kant and the true zeal for philosophy awakened by him, sophists arose, who, *invita Minerva*, first wearied out the thinking power of their time with a great deal of noise and barbarous mysterious speech, then scared it away from philosophy, and brought the study into discredit. But an avenger will again appear, who, armed with a mightier power, will restore philosophy to all her honours.'

This was throwing the gauntlet not only at Hegel's feet, but at those of all the lesser and greater lights that shone around him. Without disparagement of the uncompromising honesty, fearlessness, and love of abstract truth that prompted such utterances, surely these diatribes damaged the very cause Schopenhauer wished to serve. Verily he might have hidden his lamp of truth a little more under its bushel, without harming either it or himself, and with possible benefit to those he desired to aid. Were remarks like these likely to be agreeable?

'People like Fichte, Schelling, or Hegel, should be shut out from the ranks of philosophers, as of yore the dealers and money-changers were cast out of the Temple.'

'Hegel's philosophy is just calculated for the specious wisdom pronounced *ex cathedra*, inasmuch as instead of thoughts it contains mere words, and the boys want words to copy and take home with them; they do not want thoughts. Added to this that their results do not differ from the axioms of the natural religion, which all have imbibed with their mother's milk; it must therefore please them greatly to encounter these again in a tortuous, showy, bombastic, *galiamatias* of words. *Nihil novum sub sole!* The same charlatanry of impressing by mere nonsense, which the Schellingites introduced, and which culminates in Hegel, has been accurately described by Giordano Bruno, Opp., Vol ii., p. 282. A fitting motto for Hegel's writings is Shakespeare's "Such stuff as madmen tongue, and brain not." Cymbeline, Act v.,. Scene iv.'

Schopenhauer's opposition to the established religion was furthermore calculated to bring him into conflict with the authorities, whose main efforts were directed towards restraining open dissent at any cost. That he was thoroughly in earnest in this desire to propagate the truth, the carefully planned outlines of his lectures would show, were not the inborn and characteristic earnestness of the man sufficient guarantee that this must inevitably prove the case.

It is nevertheless curious that no students were attracted by Schopenhauer's admirable delivery and his clear pregnant mode of presenting ideas ; that no intellectual band, however tiny, was forthcoming, whose suffrages were won by his eloquent originality and self- confidence. The fact speaks for the aridity of the intellectual waste in which his lines were cast, and 'the pity of it' should throw a charitable veil over the philosopher's increasing acerbity. It was hard that, ready nerved and girded for the fight, capable and dauntless, he should be debarred the battle-field.

Ill success only contributed to exalt his self-esteem, in place of lowering it.

'How highly was Plato esteemed by his contemporaries? ' he asks, sardonically.

'My contemporaries, by entire neglect of my work, and by extolling the mediocre and bad, have done all in their power to make me distrust myself. Fortunately they have not succeeded in this, or I should have left off working, as I should have been obliged to do, had I been forced to earn my living by my labours.'

Yet as term by term his lecture-room was emptier, he became more bitter and caustic. Berlin, its dust, its glare, its bad living, grew more and more detestable, when a circumstance occurred that would have envenomed the sojourn of a person less inclined to misanthropy. He lived in lodgings, and landladies plagued and robbed him as they do minor mortals. He hated all disturbance, despised all gossip and needless chatter. With horror he discovered that an acquaintance of his landlady's was in the habit of holding coffee parties— peculiarly German feminine institutions, sacred to smalltalk, backbiting, and all uncharitableness—in *his* anteroom, in the very precincts of the philosophic temple. In an excess of blind fury, he seized her roughly and threw her out of the door. She fell on her right arm,, and was severely injured, so that she declared herself incapable of earning her livelihood. The matter was brought into court, and hotly contested by Schopenhauer on the score of infringement of his house rights. He lost his suit, and was condemned to maintain her for life. The old woman was blessed with a tough constitution, and exemplified the proverbial longevity of annuitants. Even the cholera grappled with her in vain ; for over twenty years was Schopenhauer saddled with this burden. When she departed at last, and he received the certificate of death, he wrote upon it the pun : *Obit anus, obit onus.*

As soon as the law-suit was ended, Schopenhauer shook the dust of Berlin from his feet, and fled back to Italy, thankful to leave Germany and its irksome atmosphere behind him. This time the stock of hope he carried across the Alps was scantier, his contempt for men and life more considerable.

'There are many beautiful landscapes in the world, but the *staffage* is everywhere deficient, therefore we must not let ourselves be detained by it,' he writes, amid the scenery of Vevay. Switzerland he compares felicitously to a grand and beautiful genius, barren of productive fruit.

This second Italian journey has no annals. He appears to have returned in the summer of 1823, as entries in his note books are dated Munich, in June of that year. He visited the Salzkammergut, and returned to Dresden in 1824, where he spent some time. Obstinate indifference still reigned concerning 'Die- Welt als Wille und Vorstellung.' Schopenhauer attributed to malevolence what sprung from ignorance ; his melancholy increased to mortification. He had given an ungrateful world a great immortal work, it would not regard it : he would write no more. But as he himself says:

'A man highly endowed with intellect leads, besides the individual life common to all, another that is purely intellectual, which consists in the constant enlargement, progress and development, not only of knowledge, but also of comprehension and insight, This life remains unaffected by any casualties that may befall his personality, so long as these do not disturb its workings ; therefore it lifts a man above fortune and its mutations.'

Schopenhauer was such a person ; his indignation did not overpower his reason, and his mental activity soon recommenced its efforts for the good of humanity. He turned to translation, and set on foot a negotiation for rendering Hume into German. There was an elective affinity in mind and misfortune between the two philosophers ; Hume's first efforts, like Schopenhauer's, had been condemned to obscurity. 'Out of every page of David Hume's, there is more to be learnt than out of the philosophical works of Hegel, Herbart, and Schleier-macher, all put together,' he writes, in the third edition of 'Die Welt als Wille und Vorstellung,' where he lauds in high terms the 'Natural History of Religion,' and the 'Dialogues on Natural Religion.' He laid special stress upon the latter, because they furnish cogent arguments for the miserable condition of the world, and the untenability of all optimistic ideas, although deduced from different premises to his own. The project was abandoned, which may be justly regretted in Germany, since the extant specimens of his power as a translator prove him to have been unusually gifted in this respect. A preface intended for the work, and written at Dresden in 1824, admirably reflects the philosopher's mental state.

PREFACE TO TRANSLATION OF HUME'S WORKS.

'I scarcely venture to lay before the enlightened philosophical public of our day this new German rendering of Hume's popular philosophic writings, because this public stands upon an eminence from which it not only looks down upon the once famous French philosophers such as D'Alembert, Diderot, Voltaire, Rousseau with evident contempt, as narrow and obstinate talkers, but ranks the English of the last centuries as little higher.

'Neither can there be any doubt that Hume would have spared himself the trouble of setting forth in lengthy discussions and dialogues, sceptical arguments against the chief truths of natural religion, and then again conducting their defence ; wearily weighing reasons and counter-reasons, and thus constructing a firm foundation for the belief in these truths,—he would have spared himself this trouble, if the brilliant philosophical discovery of our day had been already made in his time. I mean the important discovery that understanding comes from perceiving, and is therefore the power of perceiving, and especially of perceiving revelations of the transcendent and god-like, which dispenses with the necessity of all reflection and reasoning on such subjects. Therefore I acknowledge that I do not lay this translation before my philosophic contemporaries as a book for instruction, but only as a means for better measuring their own greatness and the height of their own standpoint, that they may the more perfectly appreciate the same.

Zu sehen wie vor tins ein weiser Mann gedacht,

Und wie wir's denn zuletzt so herrlich weit gebraeht.[5]

'The same holds good with regard to his diction. Doubtless had Hume had the good fortune to live till our present philosophic period, he would have improved his style, he would have cast aside that terseness, lucidity, precision, and attractive liveliness which are natural to him, and endeavoured to spread a mysterious darkness over his writings. By means of heavy involved periods, out of the way expressions, and self-made words, he would first have puzzled his readers, and as they continued their perusal, would have made them wonder how it was possible to read so much without gaining one single idea. This must make them feel that the less the text makes them think, the more the author, must have thought. Therefore in this respect also, the philosophic reader of our time will have the satisfaction of looking back with gratified pride on this Coryphaeus of a past period.

'Now as to what has called me to this little work. It is merely this, that since my stay in England when a boy, the English language is very easy to me ; and I have a great deal of spare time ; as I consider myself excused from working out my own thoughts for communication, for experience has verified what I had already foreseen and predicted, that such would find no readers among my contemporaries.'

In 1825 Schopenhauer returned to Berlin, and once more inscribed his name for lectures, which were, however, not even attempted. He withdrew more into himself, nourishing his rancour and contempt in solitude ; reading and studying with ardour for his own gratification, not for the world's. Learning Spanish filled up these last years at Berlin, and when he had advanced sufficiently he translated Balthasar Gracian's 'Oraculo manual y arte de prudencia,' which has been published since his death. The code of life-rules set up by this vain, witty, clever Jesuit, who sheltered his worldly views behind the name of his secular brother Lorenzo, were peculiarly calculated to interest Schopenhauer. His executors have done well to rescue the translation from MS. oblivion, since Gracian's works are too little known.

Some time passed, and still neglect was his portion : he was beginning to think of quitting Berlin ; not to settle at another university that his pride would not permit, but to leave the unpleasant place behind him, and seek a more agreeable climate. The final stroke to his vacillation came from without; in 1831 the cholera Invaded Berlin, and he fled.[6] The mere idea of any contagious disease called forth his almost insane nervousness, a tendency inherited from the father, and deeply regretted and fiercely resisted by the son. In vain. Such periods of blind terror would seize him at various times during his life, and then nothing would do but to submit. Thus he fled from Naples when the small-pox broke out there, and thus at Verona was he haunted by the idea that he had imbibed poisoned snuff. As a youth he was pursued by the fear of law suits ; for years he dreaded a criminal prosecution about the housekeeper business ; while a student he had imagined himself consumptive. These panics, heightened by a lively imagination, made such periodical attacks of horror a burden to him. At this juncture he turned his attention to Southern Germany, and selected Frankfort among its cities, solely on account of its reputation for salubrity. The town had been always spared during pestilential visitations, the living there was good, the people had some notion of comfort, and the climate to his mind stood with regard to Berlin as Milan to Frankfort. His mother's definition of the place did not deter him. 'It is too large for a little town, too small for a large one, and on the whole a gossip's nest ; a definition true to this day.

During the last years of his Berlin residence Schopenhauer was acquainted with Alexander von Humboldt, for whom he had felt great reverence as a name, but whose personality disappointed him. ' I only found great talent where I looked for genius ; *scientia* where I expected *sapientia* He also appears to have known Chamisso, since he records the poet's repeated admonitions that he should not paint the devil so black, a good grey would suffice. But black had grown ingrain by this time, and like Byron's Satan :

Where he gazed, a gloom pervaded space.

He had not been long at Frankfort before he sunk into so sombre and saturnine a mood, that for weeks he could not be induced to speak a word. His doctor imperatively enjoined a change of residence. Schopenhauer moved to the neighbouring town of Mannheim, and stayed there a whole year. It is not likely that that mathematically planned and monotonous town enlivened him ; excepting its excellent theatre, it could present no attractions. Early in 1833 he determined to return to Frankfort ; then, just about to leave, he was seized with one of his unaccountable attacks of panic. He did leave, however, and after this return never again quitted the city.

His feelings during these years of waiting for recognition are best gathered from extracts from his notebooks.

'The coldness and neglect with which I was received might have made me misdoubt myself and all that I have ever attempted ; but fortunately at the same time I heard the trumpet of fame proclaiming the entirely worthless, the palpably bad, the void of sense, as excellent, as the very acme of human wisdom. Now I saw my way and was quite satisfied, because I recognised the truth of Byron's words as to success : those who succeed will console me for my own failure.'

'The number of years that elapse between the appearance of a book and its acknowledgment, gives the measure of time that the author is in advance of his age ; perhaps it is the square or even cube root of the latter, or perhaps the time which the book has to live.'

'I have lifted the veil of truth higher than any mortal before me. But I should like to see the man who could boast of a more miserable set of contemporaries than mine.'

'The entire neglect which my work has experienced proves that either I was unworthy my age, or my age of me. In both cases one can only say : "the rest is silence." '

'There is no philosophy in the period between Kant and myself, only mere university charlatanism. Whoever reads these scribblers has lost just so much time as he has spent over them.'

'Could any great mind have reached his goal and created a lasting work, if he had taken the flitting will-o'-the-wisp of public opinion as his guiding star, *i.e.*, the opinion of little minds?'

'It enters my mind as little to mix in the philosophic disputes of the day, as to go down and take part when I see the mob having a scuffle in the street.'

'Life passes quickly, and your comprehension is slow : therefore I shall not live to see my fame, and my reward is lost.'

'He who stands alone on a height to which the others cannot ascend, must descend to them if he does not wish to be alone.'

'We often hear of the republic of learning, but never of the republic of genius. It happens thus in the latter. One giant calls to another through the weary space of centuries, without the world of dwarfs which crawls below hearing more than sound, and perceiving more than that something is going on. Besides, these dwarfs carry on endless buffoonery and make a great noise, adorn themselves with what the giants have dropped, proclaim heroes who are dwarfs themselves, and such like, while the giant spirits do not let themselves be disturbed, but continue their lofty converse.'

'Study to acquire an accurate and connected view of the utter despicability of mankind in general, then of your own contemporaries and the German scholars in particular ; then you will not stand with your work in your hand and say : "Is the world mad or I?"'

'There is nothing rarer than an original opinion, but least of all must we look for it from the learned by profession. The narrow space of their head is filled up with the traditional, and to this all original thought seems dangerous. What may the man expect who is to earn his fame for original thought from those who could never think themselves, who seek to make up for this deficiency by the traditional, of which they are the guardians. Shall we hope that an unprejudiced youth is growing up, and that there are exceptions ? Exceptions are only for exceptions, and in a world of rascals like this one must live exceptionally.'

CHAPTER VIII - HIS RESIDENCE AT FRANKFORT

THIS removal marks an epoch in Schopenhauer's history. From that day he led the anchorite life of uniform study and seclusion that gained him such nicknames as the 'Whimsical Fool of Frankfort,' 'the Modern Ascetic,' 'the Misanthrope of Frankfort,' and finally, as his fame dawned, 'the Sage.' Then came the time when his hastily striding figure was regarded as one of the city's sights, and the landlord of the Hotel d'Angleterre, where he dined, when asked if he harboured royal heads, replied, 'Yes, Dr. Schopenhauer.'

But these days were still distant when he moved his household goods to the free imperial city, with the determination henceforward to live *for* not *by* philosophy. He contended that until now it had been impossible to him to make allowance for the pettiness and despicability of mankind, and the disproportion of his moral and intellectual measuring-scale to individual reality confirmed his morose estimate of society. The desire to communicate with his fellows was as strong in him as in others ; it was his keen disappointment at finding few, if any, sympathetic souls, that drove him to sullen silence and disgust. Yet with all his hard speeches against his human brethren, his heart was sound; no hand was more open or readier than his to help any case of distress. He was careful of his property, which he administered with great prudence, insomuch that before his death he had almost doubled his capital; he held extravagance a greater sin than avarice, but he was not stingy. He supported his impoverished relations for many years, and genuine misery never appealed to him in vain. He held the fundamental basis of morality to be love of one's neighbour, and to this he traced back all virtues. His ethics were thus in unison with those of the New Testament, and might be defined as its scientific expression. His sympathies extended beyond humanity to the brute creation : he was one of the first in Germany to enforce the duty of commiseration for animals. He held that the recognition of the animal's kinship to mankind had been derived from Asia, and it exasperated him to hear of missionaries despatched to India under the plea of preaching a religion of gentleness to a people by whom its obligations were better known and more faithfully observed. The Pope's recent dictum, that it is a 'theological error to suppose that man owes any duty to animals,' would have filled him with horror. He would have proscribed animal food had he not wisely recognised that our climate necessitated such diet. According to his theory, man, in his original state, was black, and intended to live in the south, where a vegetable diet is practicable. The urgency of civilisation had pushed him northward, blanched his skin, and made him carnivorous. Yet surely, he pleaded, if we must fain live on our four- footed brethren, can we not procure them an easy death by means of chloroform? He counted it among the glories of Englishmen that they had organised a society such as that of 'Prevention of Cruelty to Animals,' and was himself an energetic promoter of similar schemes in Germany. This want of regard for the mute creation he declared a Jewish error transferred to the Christian religion.

His hatred of the Judaic element was as strong as that of his master Kant; he branded Jews as confirmed optimists, and traced Spinoza's optimism, his *vivere, agere, suum utile qucerere*, to this root. 'The Jews,' he said, 'are all more cheerful as a rule than other peoples, notwithstanding the heavy pressure that lies on them; they are a joyous nation, full of love for life. Spinoza was always cheerful.' This dictum is open to question. Schopenhauer held it with obstinate persistency, and recurs to it perpetually in his writings. Not until these Jewish doctrines were uprooted, and the people made to understand their affinity to animals, could a cessation of cruelty to the inferior creation be anticipated.

'When I was studying at Göttingen,' he says, in the 'Parerga,' 'Blumenbach spoke to us very seriously in the College of Physiology about the horrors of vivisection, and explained what a cruel and terrible thing it is, therefore we ought to employ it very seldom and only in very important experiments of actual utility. Then, too, it ought to take place with all publicity in the great auditory, and an invitation sent to all the medical students, so that this cruel sacrifice on the altar of science might be of the greatest possible utility. Nowadays, every dabbler in surgery thinks himself permitted to practise the most horrible cruelty to animals in his own torture-chamber, to decide problems whose solution has long been written in books he is too lazy or too ignorant to read. Our doctors have no longer the same classical culture as formerly, when it gave them a certain humanity and an elevated manner. Now they go as soon as possible to the university, where they only want to learn surgery, so that they may prosper on earth.'

From the first, Schopenhauer held himself more aloof from society at Frankfort than he had done in other places. This will scarcely surprise any one acquainted with the arid social conditions of that narrow-minded city, not extinct even now that it forms a mere unit in a mighty whole. Then it was an independent autonomous city; proud, arrogant, self-concentrated, devoted to the acquisition of wealth. A purely mercantile atmosphere pervaded it, little calculated to attract a thinker. Nevertheless he did not refuse interest to local concerns when they deserved attention. In 1837 a committee had been formed to erect a monument to Goethe in this, his native city. Schopenhauer took up the matter warmly, and submitted a plan for approval which, though not adopted, was excellent. He contended that men who had worked for humanity with their whole being, with heart and head, and limbs such as rulers, generals, statesmen, orators, reformers should be represented as entire figures in public monuments; while on the contrary poets, philosophers, and scholars, who had only served with their heads, should be honoured merely by busts. In support of his views he quoted the ancients. He also held it fitting to place such monuments in retired, not busy spots. Another of his proposals, to mark the house where Goethe was born with a tablet, was adopted.

His outer life settled down into a uniform routine, never again abandoned. It is described by his friend Dr. Gwinner, and is, though less ascetic, not dissimilar in essentials to that of his master, Kant. Blessed with a sound constitution, nothing ever interfered to interrupt methodical adherence to his self-imposed rules, when he had once recognised them as beneficial. He was no friend to the early bird, and contended that all who worked their brain need much repose. Nine hours was a fair and not unreasonable amount of sleep. Still he knew the value of the morning hours, and did not waste them in inordinate slumber. He got up between seven and eight, both summer and winter, and took a cold sponge bath, at that time a phenomenon in Germany, whither the use of the matutinal tub is only just slowly penetrating. When he was dressed he partook of coffee, which he prepared himself. His housekeeper was strictly forbidden to show herself; he held every interruption at that time as dangerous to the brain, which he compared to a freshly-tuned instrument. In this concentrated mental mood he applied himself to writing ; at first he devoted the whole morning to this, later only three hours, after which he would receive visitors. As he was apt to forget time in the flow of conversation, his housekeeper had orders to put in an appearance punctually at midday, and this was a signal for his guests to depart. After playing the flute as a half- hour's relaxation, he dressed with scrupulous care in tailcoat and white tie, and proceeded to the Hôtel d'Angleterre to dine at the *table-d'hotê*. Though he did this all his life, he could not reconcile himself to the disadvantages of the custom ; the noise of the guests, the rattling of the plates, the servility of the waiters. As he grew deafer he suffered less from this. He was a hearty eater, and would have endorsed Sir Arthur Helps's observation that philosophers generally have good appetites. Kant and Goethe had also been large eaters, and his dietetic maxim was that consumption of force and supply must exist in the same ratio.

'Sir,' he said one day to a stranger who watched him attentively across the table, ' Sir, you are astonished at my appetite. True, I eat three times as much as you, but then I have three times as much mind.'

He held conversation at meal-times as good for digestion, but had frequently to refrain from want of worthy companions. For a long time he was in the habit of placing a gold piece beside his plate at the commencement of dinner, and replacing it in his pocket at the end. This strange proceeding aroused curiosity. 'That piece of gold,' he explained, is to go to the poor, whenever I hear the officers discuss anything more serious than women, dogs, and horses.' He was fond of talking, and talked extremely well. As he grew well known people frequently came to the one o'clock *table-d'hotê* to see him, and if he found intelligence he would willingly allow himself to be drawn out. Dr. Gwinner relates how greatly he was struck with this when he first saw him. 'He was a glaring violation of his own doctrine of the nullity of individual life, since he was altogether a person when he spoke, and the more deeply he thought the more individual he became. I was very young when I first heard him speak. I sat near him at the table-d'hotê, but did not know him, nor who he was. He was demonstrating the rudiments of logic to some one, and I vividly recall the strange impression it made on me to hear a person talk of $a = a$ with an expression of countenance as though he were speaking with his beloved of love.' Yet however deeply engrossed, he never forgot external things ; if his dog wished to be let in or out of the room, he would immediately spring up in the midst of the most abstract talk, gratify the creature's will, and then resume the thread unbroken.

After dinner he returned home, partook of coffee, and slept for an hour. He then devoted himself to reading lighter literature ; towards evening he went for a walk, no matter what weather. If possible he chose lonely field paths ; only the very worst weather forced him to remain in the confines of the town. His reason for walking fast he found in Aristotle's axiom that life consists of motion, ὁ βίος ἐν τῇ κινήσει ἐστι. In the 'Parerga' he counsels a two hours' walk as necessary for health ; all the more important for those whose occupations are sedentary. His dog, a white poodle called Atma (i. e. Soul of the World) accompanied him. This dog became as well known as his master, and children passing the philosopher's rooms would remark : 'We saw young Schopenhauer looking out of the window.' He smoked while he walked, but always threw away his cigar when half consumed, as he held the moist end to be unwholesome. He would strike his cane impatiently on the ground, and utter inarticulate grunts at times, looking neither to right or left, and failing to recognise the acquaintances he passed. This was due in a measure to his shortsightedness : glasses he thought noxious to the eyes—man's greatest treasure—and avoided wearing them as much as possible. If people gave way to him in the street, passing to the left, his anger burst bounds. 'The idiots, can they never learn to keep to the right!' Even such trifles would lead him to philosophize, for he sought reasons for all things, great and small.

'To a German, order, rules and laws are hateful in everything ; he has a tender regard for individual bent and his own caprice, tempered with more or less of reason according to the strength of his reasoning powers. Therefore I doubt whether the Germans will ever learn, what every Briton in the United Kingdom and the Colonies invariably practises, always to keep to the right when walking in the street.'

His inattention to passers-by gained him the reputation of incivility; his mutterings raised suspicions that he was ridiculing those he passed. Hearing this, he made a point of lifting his hat to any person who raised theirs, whether he knew them or no.' Give the world its due in bows,' he said. He preferred to take his walks alone.

'Ah yes, you like walking alone,' an empty-headed officer once said to Schopenhauer. ' Well so do I. Let us walk together.' Schopenhauer's horror at this truly Irish proposal was great. He craved solitude to enjoy communion with Nature and observe her workings. 'Every spot that is entirely uncultivated, wild, and left to itself, however small it may be, if the paw of man will but spare it, will be ornamented by Nature in the most tasteful way. She adorns it with plants, flowers, and bushes, whose unconstrained natural grace and charming grouping plainly show that they have not grown up under the scourge of the great egotist.'

Schopenhauer always looked forward to spring ; and, as its herald, he welcomed the closed catkins of the hazel, gathering them and placing them in luke-warm water, that they might open quickly and strew their pollen on his table. He occasionally suffered his disciples to accompany him on these promenades. One of them has left a piteous record of a chase under a melting July sun, Schopenhauer meanwhile philosophizing hard, and the poor listener striving to catch every pearl that fell from his lips, and yet not expire under the combined exertion. Subjects for philosophy were furnished by any external incident; such as the gait of the people they met, which Schopenhauer would mimic to perfection. He hated an awkward carriage, and saw in it a connection with the functions of the brain.

'It is physiologically remarkable, that the preponderance in mass of the brain over the spine and the nerves, which, according to Sömmering's ingenious theory, is the most accurate index of the degree of intelligence, as well for animals as for men, also directly increases the mobility and agility of the limbs, because by the great inequality of proportion, the dependence of all the motor nerves upon the brain becomes more decided. Besides, the cerebellum, the real director of movements, has a part in the qualitative completeness of the large brain ; thus, by means of both, all voluntary movements acquire greater delicacy, velocity, and agility. From the concentration of the centre of all activity arises what Lichtenbergpraises in Garrick, that *he* seemed present in every muscle of his body. Thus heaviness in movement of the body points to heaviness in thoughts, and like insensibility of feature and dulness of expression, is considered, in individuals and in nations, as a mark of want of intellect. Another symptom of the physiological connection is the circumstance that many persons, when conversation begins to interest them, are immediately obliged to stand still, because as soon as their brain has to connect a few ideas, they no longer have the strength to keep their legs in motion by the motor nerves. So scantily is everything meted out to them.'

The latter characteristic, referred to by Schopenhauer, is regarded by Englishmen, with some show of truth, as essentially a foreign habit, in which case Schopenhauer's philosophical explanation falls to the ground. He further contends that perhaps 'it might be possible to distinguish, even from behind, a dunce, a fool, and a man of intellect. The leaden dulness of all his movements marks the dunce, stupidity sets her seal on every gesture ; while intellect and thought do the same. The cause of this is in great part that the larger and more developed the brain, and the thinner in proportion the spinal cord and the nerves, the greater will be not only the intelligence, but also the mobility and pliancy of all the limbs, because they are more directly and entirely governed by the brain : thus everything depends on one thread. Every movement plainly marks its purpose.'

In summer Schopenhauer often took walking day- tours, but always returned to sleep. He had lost all taste for travelling, and thought it as unnecessary for age as needful for youth. In the modern love of travel he beheld a revival of the nomadic instinct, prevalent in the lowest stages of civilisation, and reappearing in the highest : analogous, with the exception that need formed the spur for the former, *ennui* for the latter. After his walk, he went to the reading room to glance over the 'Times' and some English and French reviews. Then he would generally attend a concert or theatre. When he grew too deaf this pleasure was greatly curtailed, and he had to confine himself to well- known symphonies, oratorios, or operas ; plays became impossible. Beethoven was his favourite composer, and if a symphony of his was followed by the work of another musician, he left the concert room rather than allow his pleasure to be distracted. The music of the future he condemned after the first hearing of the 'Flying Dutchman.' 'Wagner does not know what music is,' was his verdict ; the more interesting, because it happens that Wagner is one of Schopenhauer's most ardent followers, and Wagner's disciples contend that Schopenhauer's theories of music are the only ones that adequately explain their master's ideas. Apparently they never met, but Schopenhauer mentions in one of his letters, dated Frankfort, December 30th, 1854 :—

'This was followed by a book of Richard Wagner's, which was not printed for the trade, but only for friends, on beautiful thick paper, and neatly bound. It is called, "Der King der Nibelungen," and is the first of a series of four operas which he means to compose some day. I suppose they are to be the real work of art of the future. It seems very phantastic : I have as yet only read the prelude, shall see further on. He sent no letter, only wrote in the book : "With reverence and gratitude." '

After his evening recreation Schopenhauer supped ; this meal he again partook at the hotel, when he was often very approachable, and would converse far into the night with pleasant companions. His supper was frugal, some cold meat and half a bottle of light wine. Wine easily excited him ; after the second glass he was more animated ; he was inclined to consider it a test against a man's intellectual powers, if he could stand much spirituous drink. For beer he had a veritable disgust. When no society was forthcoming, he returned home, lit his pipe, and read. He smoked a five-foot- long pipe, not from bravado like a student, but because he held it less noxious, since the smoke got cooled in this long passage. Before he retired to bed he would read the Oupnekhat. 'There was more to be learnt out of one page of these ancient Vedic books, than out of ten volumes of the post-Kantian philosophers.' He called it his Bible. 'The Oupnekhat is the most grateful and elevating reading it is possible to have on this earth ; the book has been the comfort of my life and will also be that of my death.' It turned his mind to serious thoughts before sleeping. Then, slipping tinder the light coverlet he held ample both for winter and summer, he at once sank into the deep slumber proverbially enjoyed by the righteous.

His apartment was extremely simple, and resembled a *pied à terre* rather than a permanent home. He had no aesthetic sense for furnishing and external luxury. Until long past fifty, he had no furniture of his own. The prominent characteristic of his room was a gilt statue of Buddha, that stood on his writing-table next to a bust of Kant. Over his sofa hung an oil portrait of Goethe, besides portraits of Kant, Shakespeare, Descartes, and Claudius, and innumerable engravings of dogs, A black bearskin marked the resting-place of Atma, or his poodle predecessors and ancestors. The house in which he lodged, in the Schone Aussicht, now bearing a tablet recording the fact, overlooked Sachsenhausen, the suburb of Frankfort, famed for the gross incivility of its population. With his own fondness for strong expressions, this *vis-a-vis* gave him peculiar pleasure, as also the circumstance that it was exactly opposite the many-windowed Deutsch Ordenshaus, the home of that mysterious personage 'der Franckforter,' author of the 'Theologia Germanica,' a favourite book, in which Schopenhauer saw wonderful analogies to his own doctrines. 'I am the first,' he said, 'to reach my hand to him across five hundred years : so far apart do people stand in history.'

Schopenhauer's works so literally bristle and overflow with quotations, that he has obtained the fame of an omnivorous reader. This is by no means the case. He did not read much, and only such works as bore upon the subjects uppermost in his mind. He condemned reading too much and at wrong times, but especially reading the ephemeral literature of the day, instead of the imperishable works of the great minds of all ages. He inveighed against the stupid public who neglect the noblest, rarest minds of every kind, for the scribblings of commonplace brains, which appear, like the flies, every year in countless numbers. He attached great importance to the art of not reading. It consists in leaving unregarded the literature of the day, so beloved by the public ; he censured the prejudice that thinks the newest book the best, as though the last spoken word were always the worthiest, and the last written book an improvement on what preceded. An excellent old book has often been set aside for a new and worse one. Schopenhauer explained the absence of bad writings among the classics, by the fact that writing books was not with the ancients a branch of industry ; they did not, therefore, like the moderns, carry the dregs to market when the spirit had evaporated. Writing books for the sake of making money he held the ruin of literature ; he disliked the laudatory remarks appended to advertisements, and strictly forbade such to accompany his writings. 'It is highly improper to make a display of one's titles and dignities on a title-page ; in literature, none but intellectual advantages should be considered. Whoever employs others, shows that he lacks these.' He thought anonymity a shield for literary knavery, that it often hid nothing but obscurity, incompetence, and mediocrity. The condition of liberty of the press should be rigid interdiction of all anonymous and pseudonymous authorship, so that everyone may at least be responsible with his honour for what he proclaims through the far-reaching trumpet of the press. He thought it dishonorable to attack anyone anonymously who had not himself written anonymously, and was a sworn foe to cliquism and mutual admiration. He thought it pernicious to extend to literature the toleration shown by society to stupid, brainless people, for there they are impertinent intruders, and it is a duty towards the good to attack the bad. In literature politeness is an alien, often a dangerous, element.

Attentive readers of Schopenhauer's works will find a constant reference to the same authors. As a mere youth, he had already restricted his reading to certain principal works, giving time to few modern authors.

'It occurs to me as little to acquaint myself with all the philosophic essays of my contemporaries, as it would occur to a man, travelling from capital to capital on important business, to seek acquaintance with the dignitaries and aristocrats of each little town *en route*?

He read slowly and carefully, marking the passages that struck him, and adding marginal annotations. The true enjoyment of a book was not found for him till the second reading, when a cursory survey would yield its quintessence. While reading he was always producing, and for this cause alone he held the choice of literature of great importance. His excellent memory helped him to retain the substance of books : still he held individual thought more important. Much reading is pernicious, because the continuous stream of foreign ideas hinders original ones, and cripples the mental powers. He even held it dangerous to read on a subject before meditating upon it, because the alien treatment of the matter enters the brain with the new material. While reading, the mind is forced by this external agent to attend to some subject to which it may not at that moment incline, while in individual thought it follows its own bent. We ought only to read when the spring of thought has ebbed. It is a sin against the intellect to repress our own gushing thoughts by taking up a book. It is like looking at a herbarium, or pictures,, instead of Nature herself. We can force ourselves to read, but not to think. We should therefore do well to use that time for reading when we are not disposed for thinking.

The Greek and Roman authors were through life his intimate acquaintances, especially Aristotle, Plato, and Seneca. Books dealing with books, such as critical analyses and translations, were his peculiar horror ; he detested and suspected all knowledge acquired at second-hand, and demanded that every student desirous of real scholarship should at least know Latin. He was rather fond of translating himself, and the marginalia of his German poets contain many renderings into English, some of them singularly happy, as this from the Prologue to Faust. A terser version has never yet been penned :

I like to see the old one now and then,

And do t' avoid a rupture all I can ;

In a great Lord, forsooth, its very civil,

To speak humanely even to the devil.

The only book he liked to read in a translation was the Septuagint version of the Old Testament, which to his mind preserved more of the aroma of the original than the modern renderings impregnated by the tendencies of the church. English was his favourite language ; it opened for him the paths of Sanscrit and Hindoo literature, obviously of peculiar interest, as in entire conformity with his own doctrines. Every semblance of Buddhism attracted his notice ; as, for instance, the monks of La Trappe, whom he esteemed as the most worthy monastic order. Gwinner relates how deeply Schopenhauer was moved on seeing a portrait of the Abbé de Rancé. He gazed at the face long and earnestly, and then turning away with a pained look, said, 'That is a matter of grace.' Schopenhauer could not bring his nature into harmony with perfect asceticism, much as he valued the practice.

Besides the books mentioned, he liked Machiavelli's Principe, Shenstone's Works, those of the French moralists, Goethe, Shakespeare (Polonius speech to Laertes was his guiding star), Calderon, Byron, Burns, and Schiller. Of novels he upheld as the best, Don Quixote, Tristram Shandy, Heloise, and Wilhelm Meister.

Thus lonely, self-engrossed, rich in 'un grand soimémé' innocent of the very meaning of the word 'ennui, Schopenhauer passed his days. He had been near marriage several times, but always abandoned the project, partly because he did not consider his means sufficient for the maintenance of a family, partly because he did not think it would harmonise with his calling, which demanded solitude. Even in Saadi's Gulistan can be read that he who has cares for bread and butter cannot be creative. Besides, every day convinced him how few marriages really turned out well, how young men were hampered in their career by becoming drudges; how they were turned into mere bread-winners, and all their legitimate leisure absorbed in procuring leisure for their wives. The unmarried only bear half the burden of life, and a votary of the Muses must be unhampered as far as possible. 'Matrimony—War and Want,' was his maxim. He repressed the inborn yearning he held in common with all men to seek a kindred soul, recipient of his thoughts and feelings, and sang the praises of solitude until at last he grew to believe in them entirely. But a melancholy sobs through them, imperceptible in the similar utterances of Descartes, who lived as isolated amid the mercantile surroundings of Amsterdam as Schopenhauer among those of Frankfort, but Descartes' obscurity did not pain him, while Schopenhauer's did. He once acknowledged that throughout life he had felt terribly lonely, and this was not his fault, he passionately argued ; he had thrust none from him who were worthy ; he had met with none, excepting Goethe and a few others, much older than himself; the difference between his being and that of ordinary men was forced upon him, and after vainly seeking for a man and finding none, he had learnt in sorrow to love solitude. 'Were I a King,' he said, 'my prime command would be—Leave me alone.' *On a les défauts de ses qualités*, says the French writer, sadly, wittily. He suffered from his mental loneliness, the common curse of genius.

In later life Schopenhauer wrote : 'As that country is the happiest which needs few or no imports, so also the man whose inner wealth suffices him, and who requires for his entertainment little or nothing from without. Such supplies are expensive, destroy independence, are dangerous and vexatious, and in the end, only a bad substitute for native produce. Indeed, in no respect should much be expected from outside, from others. The limits are very narrow of what one man can be to another ; in the end everyone remains alone ; and it depends very greatly what manner of man he is.

Still to ourselves in every place consigned,

Our own felicity we make or find.

'Everyone must therefore be the best and most to himself; the more this is the case, and the more he thus finds the sources of enjoyment in himself, the happier will he be. Aristotle was right when he said *n svSaifjiovia T&V avrapKwv eoti*. All outward sources of happiness and enjoyment are in their very nature uncertain, precarious, transitory, and subject to chance, and even under the most favourable circumstances they may easily fail. In fact this cannot be avoided, because they are not always accessible. In old age, especially, they almost necessarily fail us ; then affection, mirth, love of travel, of horses, fitness for society, forsake us, even friends and relations are removed by death. Then that which a man has in himself is of greater importance than ever, for this will stand the longest test. But at every age it remains the true and only continuous source of happiness, for nowhere in the world is there much to be had ; it is full of want and sorrow, and those who have escaped these evils are everywhere threatened by *ennui*. Besides it is a world, in which, as a rule, wickedness has the upper hand, and folly the casting vote.

'Fate is cruel, and mankind contemptible. In a world so constituted, he who has enough in himself is like a warm, bright, cheerful room at Christmas, in the midst of the snow and ice of a December night. Therefore, the happiest, though not the most brilliant, lot on earth, is unquestionably to have a rich individuality, and especially a great deal of intellect. Queen Christina, of Sweden, when only nineteen, made a wise remark about Descartes, who had lived for twenty years in the deepest seclusion in Holland, and was then only known to her by one essay and by report. "*M. Descartes est le plus heureux de tous les hommes et sa condition* me semble digne d'envie." [7] But it is needful, as in the case of Descartes, that external circumstances should in so far favour this, that a man may possess and enjoy himself, as the Preacher says (vii. 11) "Wisdom is good with an inheritance, and is a profit to them that see the sun." Whoever has been blessed with this lot, by the favour of Nature and Fate, will watch with anxious care that the inner source of his happiness may remain accessible to him; for this, the conditions are independence and leisure. He will willingly purchase these by temperance and economy ; the rather because he is not like others, dependent on external sources of enjoyment. The desire for office?, money, favour, and the world's approbation, will not mislead him to renounce himself and submit to the low aims or the bad taste of mankind. When the circumstances arise he will act like Horace in the epistle to Maecenas (Lib. i. Ep. 7). It is foolish to lose inwardly for the sake of outward gain, *i.e.* to give up entirely, or in great part, leisure and independence, for the sake of splendour, position, show, titles, and honour. This is what Goethe did. My genius has drawn me strenuously in the other direction.'

Schopenhauer knew that only abnormal natures needed to live this abnormal life. Nature's destiny for man was labour by day, rest by night, and little leisure, wife and children to be his comfort in life and death. Where a craving for intellectual creation existed, along with a positive call to impart such creation to the world for its good, these normal conditions were suspended. A marked plan was visible in the lives of most, which lead them into the paths best suited to their individuality; be their outward conditions what they might, inborn impulse would break down all obstacles ; even opposing circumstances would be forced to work for the common end. Schopenhauer belonged to others, not to himself; he had felt this from childhood : he was destined to use his powers for the common weal, more than common leisure and freedom were therefore his due. Man's ordinary happiness consisted in changes from work to pleasure : for him these were identical. Life, for such as he, was of necessity a monodrama. A missionary of truth to mankind he had as little in common with them apart from his mission, and could fraternise with them as little, as the missionary in China with the Chinese. But as the men among whom he lived could be so little to him, he valued the monuments left by the few great ones of the earth. He compared books to a letter from home, prized more highly by the exile than any conversation with a casual bystander. Did not a traveller on a desert shore welcome more eagerly a single trace of human workmanship than the presence of monkeys and cockatoos innumerable on all the trees? The comfort afforded by intellectual monuments had never failed him throughout life, and his converse with the dead was sweetened by the thought that he too would leave behind him similar remains, destined to afford comfort and strength to generations yet unborn. At the moment of his deepest obscurity he wrote prophetically that the dayspring of fame would gild with its first rays the evening of his life, and relieve it of its gloom. Occasional outbreaks of discontent he conquered in a singular manner. After enumerating the various causes for contentment he possessed, he persuaded himself that in feeling discontent he had made an error in the person, and held himself to be some one else whose misery he was pitying ; for instance a *privat docent* who could not become professor ; a person who had been abused by a Philistine or maligned by a woman; a lover who could not obtain the maiden he desired ; an invalid forced to keep the house ; and more such like. But who, after all, was he? He was the writer of 'Die Welt als Wille und Vorstellung,' he who had solved the great problem of existence, destined to occupy the thoughts of centuries. This was he : what then could hurt him throughout the few years he had to breathe?

In this artificial form of contentment Schopenhauer's life flowed on in uniform monotony of outward events, but inwardly maturing by meditation and experience. He continued to preserve the sullen silence towards the world he held its due in return for its neglect of his great work. But fame was to dawn at last, though it only laid its wreath of roses upon his whitened hairs, as he touchingly told his friend.

CHAPTER IX - HIS DAWN OF FAME

IT was not till 1836 that Schopenhauer broke his seventeen years silence by a tract on 'The Will in Nature'; since a Latin version of his optical treatise in the 'Scriptores Opthalmologici Minores,' of Justus Eadius, published in 1831, can hardly be counted. Though never losing faith in the ultimate recognition of his philosophical significance, Schopenhauer either disdained to imitate, or despaired of imitating, the example of those teachers who have refused to be ignored, and have steadily pressed their doctrines upon the world until they have conquered a hearing by sheer dint of pertinacity. The occasion of his next public appearance was purely external: the offer by the Royal Norwegian Academy of Drontheim of a prize for the best Essay on the Freedom of the Will and the Doctrine of Philosophical Necessity. For this (1839) he was a successful competitor.

Encouraged by this first gleam of prosperity, he next year entered the lists for another premium offered by the Royal Danish Academy as the reward for the best inquiry into the grounds of moral obligation. This time he was unsuccessful, a disappointment the more galling as he had the field entirely to himself. The Danish academicians added greatly to his irritation by the issue of a document setting forth their reasons for the rejection of his essay ; in which, after somewhat inconsistently alleging, first, that he had not answered the question propounded ; and secondly, that he had answered it wrong, they wound up with a hint that no one could reasonably expect recognition as a philosopher who spoke disrespectfully of his brethren. Schopenhauer's language respecting Fichte and Hegel had certainly been far from becoming ; he now included the Danish Academy in his animosity ; and his two essays, on their appearance in 1841 under the title of 'The Two Main Problems of Ethical Science,' were garnished with a very lively polemical preface. He farther insisted that the words 'Not crowned by the Royal Danish Academy' should be printed 'in good fat letters' under the title. He continued to speak of the sages of Copenhagen with suitable contempt for the rest of his days, and would probably, with Oehlenschlager, have been ready to accept Shakespeare's dictum : [8]

You cannot speak of reason to the Dane,

without caring to look further.

In fact, both the academies had but acted in accordance with the laws naturally and infallibly operative upon learned bodies. The Norwegian Society had crowned him for defending an accepted thesis ; the Danish had condemned him for propounding a novelty. A writer on Liberty and Necessity must take one side or the other, and has ample precedent for either. Schopenhauer's essay is vigorous and perspicuous in the highest degree, but, as he himself admits, it is impossible to be more unanswerable than Priestley, from whom his arguments are mainly derived. He seeks, however, to engraft upon Priestley's demonstration that man's action is necessitated, Kant's contention that man is nevertheless responsible. The argument apparently is, that all action is the necessary product of character, but that man is responsible for his character notwithstanding. As we have already remarked, Schopenhauer does not regard character as the creation of circumstances, but as the incarnation of the impersonal Will whose blind longing for objective existence has given birth to the world of phenomena. As he himself expresses it, responsibility is *transcendent*; it is consequently transferred from the individual to the nature of things, and the ethical puzzle, why people should be punished for what they cannot help, remains as he found it.

Less brilliant and more abstruse, the second essay is more original. It is devoted in the first place to the overthrow of Schopenhauer's revered master, Kant's, theory of the categorical imperative [9] as the basis of moral obligation ; secondly, to an endeavour to establish another theory in its room. Schopenhauer lays it down that no action not wholly disinterested can be regarded as meritorious. He strives by an acute analysis to show that an action performed on the principle of behaving as one would wish one's neighbour to behave, has contracted a taint of impurity, inasmuch as it is remotely biassed by the calculation that this will in the long run prove for the interest of the agent himself. No action has any moral value in his eyes unless it is prompted by pure compassion. This theory, of course, is strictly Buddhistic, and is a natural corollary from that view of the essential evil of all existence which he shared with Buddha. In the latter part of the essay he analyses the nature of meritorious deeds and emotions, to show how they may be deduced from his cardinal principle of action.

These essays do not appear to have attracted much notice, and Schopenhauer's bitterness increased. Yet he did not cease to write, though he did not publish. The second volume of 'Die Welt als Wille und Vorstellung' was a work very near his heart, and one he desired to complete for his own satisfaction, even if he failed to satisfy the public. He worked slowly, deliberately, carefully, sparing no pains to perfect his theory. Then in May, 1843, he wrote to Brockhaus, who had published the first edition.

Frankfort, May, 1843.
'SIR, You will think it quite natural that I apply to you to offer you the publication of the second volume of 'Die Welt als Wille und Vorstellung,' which I have now completed, but you will doubtless be surprised that I have only done so after the lapse of twenty-four years. Yet the reason is simply this, that I was not able to finish it sooner, although all these years I have really been occupied ceaselessly with the preparations for this work. What is to endure long grows slowly. The actual composition has been the labour of the last four years, and I entered upon it because I saw that it was time to finish, for I have just completed my fifty- fifth year, and am thus entering upon an age where life already begins to be uncertain, and even if it continues long, the time approaches when the powers of mind lose their energy. This second volume has important advantages over the former one, and stands in relation to it as the finished picture to the mere sketch. For it has the thoroughness and riches of thought and knowledge which can only be the fruit of a whole life spent in constant study and meditation. At any rate it is the best thing I have ever written. Even the first volume will only now declare its real significance. I have also been able to express myself much more freely and easily ; partly because the present age can endure this better, partly because the years I have attained, with secured independence and determined emancipation from the university mannerism, permit me a more decided bearing. According to my calculation, this volume will equal the other in size. Yet I cannot promise this for certain ; as the very unequal use of the white spaces of the MS. [10] do not enable me to make more than an average estimate. The volume consists of fifty chapters, arranged in four books, which correspond to those in the first volume and are supplementary to them.

'Now it is my fervent wish that you should agree to print the first volume again, and thus to publish a new edition, double the size, in two volumes, so that a work whose worth and importance have as yet been acknowledged by only a few voices, appearing in a newer and worthier form, may at length attract, as it deserves, the attention of the public. This may the rather be hoped, because the humbug so long carried on by the boasted heroes of the cathedra has been more and more unmasked, and revealed in its emptiness, while at the same time the decrease of religious belief has made the need of philosophy more keenly felt than ever, and the interest in it has grown stronger and more universal, while on the other hand there is nothing to satisfy this want ; for this will never be accomplished by the works of those who in their philosophy have sought merely their own advantage. This, therefore, is the propitious moment for the revival of my work, and as by providential disposition, it comes just at the time when I have at length completed my task. The public will not always be unjust to me, as it has hitherto been. I wish you knew the real history of literature : then you would know that all really good works, all that have afterwards enjoyed a lasting reputation, were at first neglected like mine, while all the false and bad were uppermost. For these know so well how to boast, that there is no chance for the good and true, and they must fight their way to gain the light at last. My time also must and will come. The question is in fact about giving to the world a work whose worth and importance is so great that I do not venture to express it, even towards you, its publisher, because you could not believe me. But I can at least show you that it is only the cause itself I value, and that I have no by-ends in view. If you now resolve on publishing this second edition, I leave it entirely to you whether or no you will give me any honorarium for the two volumes. In the latter case you would certainly receive for nothing the work of my whole life, but I did not undertake it for money, and I have continued it till old age with iron perseverance. At the same time I know that so extensive a book must cost you a great deal for printing and paper, which will only be repaid after a long time. Your complaints about the small sale, your assurance of having destroyed many copies, remain in my memory, and have caused me much sorrow ; although I know that it was not the book, but the incapability of the public and the craftiness of the university philosophers, who lead it according to their personal wishes, which was at fault. Meanwhile, however, I do not wish you to sustain any loss through my affairs, not even if you are rich : therefore I arrange the conditions in such a manner that loss would be impossible. For I have gradually succeeded in gaining a small public for my writings. One day it will be a very large one, and my book will go through many editions, though I may not live to see it. I have already got so far in the final revision of the second volume that it will be ready for print in a month's time ; then, while you are printing the second volume, I would make some trifling alterations in the first ; these would be more considerable in the criticism of Kant's philosophy, which forms the appendix, and may thus fill up another sheet. Awaiting your reply,' &c.

The answer he received appears from his next letter.

'SIR, The refusal contained in your favour was as unexpected as it was disappointing. Still, I must decidedly refuse the proposals which you have well-meaningly made to me. It is true I wished to give the public a present, and a very valuable one, but I cannot and will not pay for it besides.... Is the notorious degeneracy of the age really so great that while Hegel's nonsense attains many editions, and the worthless philosophic jargons of a thousand commonplace brains is paid by the public, a publisher will not even venture the cost of printing on a work of mine which contains the labour of my whole life? Well then, my work shall be left alone, to appear sometime as posthumous, when the generation has come that will welcome every line of my writings. It will not fail to come.

'Meanwhile I do not regard all this as fixed and decided ; on the contrary, at present I will leave no worthy means untried of bringing to the light of day this work, completed with so much love and enthusiasm. In the first place, I offer you the second volume alone, without the first, and without honorarium, though this goes much against my wishes. You must surely see that the possessors of the first volume will take as many copies of the second volume of a work of whose worth they have understood something, as are necessary to cover the costs of printing. Besides, this volume contains the concentration of all the thoughts I have set down in the last twenty-four years, and is divided into fifty chapters, which are independent of one another and treat each of a particular philosophic subject, written in my usual manner, free from all scholastic constraint, clear, lively, and agreeable. They may be each separately read and enjoyed. They will also create a desire for the first volume, which is certainly needed for their thorough comprehension, and thus also necessitate a second edition of this. If you were here, I would show you, as an instance, the chapter which consists of about thirty-six printed pages "On the Metaphysics of Sexual Love," which traces this passion to its primal source. (Of course this would be in my house, as on account of the entire novelty of the contents, I shall give nothing out of my hands.) I will take any wager you would hesitate no longer.

'Still, if you do not accept this proposal, I must try to find a publisher how and where I can, and I do not give up the hope of doing so. Nay, I should have no doubt about it, if I did not foresee that everyone would immediately ask why you, its natural publisher, do not take it. That stands in my way and creates a difficulty, for otherwise I could not want for a publisher. If there is no clever man about you who has sufficient knowledge, understanding and impartiality, to make you aware of the worth of my work, why read what Jean Paul says of the book which you found such a bad speculation. Look at the place I occupy among the first rank of philosophers, in Rosenkranz's " History of Kant's Philosophy," or read in the *Pilot* of May, 1841, an Essay written by an entire stranger, called "Last Judgment upon Hegel's Philosophy," which speaks of me with the highest praise, and says that I am plainly the greatest philosopher of the age, which is really saying much less than the good man thinks. The want of a publisher may vex me greatly, but it cannot change my opinion of the case. Just the same happened to the great Hume—nay worse, for according to his own account, in the first year after the publication of his English History, the publisher only sold forty-five copies, and now, after eighty years, it appears afresh every few years in the original, and in translations. I read this winter in your own Conversations-Blatt that Groschen complained of the bad sale of "Iphigenie" and "Egmont," and that "Wilhelm Meister" would not sell at all. But the newspaper, *Die Lokomotive*, sells 8000 copies daily; that shows the relation between value and demand. Still I do not in any way reproach you for speaking from your own standpoint as I do from mine ; you cannot live by posterity. Therefore I once more await your decision, and remain, &c.'

This letter remained unanswered, whereupon Schopenhauer wrote the following.

'Sir, On the 17th instant I had the honour of writing to you according to your wish, and making you a final proposal. To my surprise I am still without an answer. As I cannot fancy you would leave my letter disregarded, I am in doubt whether it is my letter to you, or your reply, that has not come to hand. Therefore I beg you to relieve my doubt, and in case my second proposal should please you as little as my first, at least to tell me so in two words, that I may take other steps in my concerns. In the meantime the idea has occurred to me of giving my work another form, and letting it appear independently.'

Brockhaus replied to this letter, saying he had changed his determination, and would undertake the work. Upon which Schopenhauer replied.

'June 14th.
'SIR, The announcement of the change in your determination has given me much pleasure. I acknowledge this candidly, but just as candidly I assure you of my firm conviction that you will not be doing a bad business by undertaking my work, but rather a very good one, so that the day may come when you will laugh heartily at your hesitation to risk the cost of printing. What is truly and earnestly meant is often very slow, but always sure to gain way, and remains afterwards in continued esteem. The great soap-bubble of the Fichte-Schelling-Hegel philosophy is at length about to burst; at the same time, the need of philosophy is greater than ever ; more solid nourishment will now be sought, and this is only to be found in me, the despised, because I am the only one who has wrought from an inward call.

'We are therefore agreed on the chief point. ... As I mentioned in my first letter, I have some alterations to make in the first volume, and especially some important additions to the criticism on Kant's philosophy. . . . This will require time, as I work *con amore*, and therefore slowly, and it is a rule of mine never to write except in the first three morning hours, because the brain has then its best energy and clearness. . . .

'The whole, in one volume, would make so large and thick a book that it would not be possible to hold it in reading, a disagreeable annoyance ; or the print would be so small that it would hurt the eyes, and would frighten off many, especially elderly people. For there is material for two thick volumes. . . . For the contract I propose the following easy conditions. . . .

'5thly. You will promise to send me every sheet for the third correction, with the piece of MS. belonging to it, and not to print the sheet before it has come back with my correction and signature. I care more about this point than any other, and to my great joy I see that you yourself wish it. Only let it stand in the contract, for my satisfaction, for I have not yet got over the printer's mistakes in the first edition. I am very exact in my corrections. The courier post, which carries the light parcels for the post-waggon, takes only forty hours between Frankfort and Leipzig. It arrives here daily at half-past ten in the morning, and it leaves again at ten in the evening ; so that I have plenty of time for the correcting, and you get back the sheet within seventy-two hours. I promise faithfully to correct each sheet without delay, and despatch it again the same day. It is indispensable that the MS. should accompany each sheet, as I know from experience. I suppose I need not return that.

'6thly. You must promise not to add to the advertisements of the book any praise or other comment. I have a great objection to it.

'7thly. I wish to have ten copies for myself.'

Having thus settled affairs with the publisher, Schopenhauer in his foresight also furnished the printer with special directions. The letter is highly characteristic.

'My dear Printer,

'We are related to one another as the body is to the soul, and must, like these, labour in unison, so that a work may be completed which shall bring honour to the master. I have done my part towards this, and at every line, every word, every letter, I have thought of you, and whether you would be able to read it. Now do your part. My MS. is not elegant, but very legible, and written in large characters. Much revision and diligent filing have led to many corrections and insertions, but everything is clear, and the reference to each insertion exact by marks, so that you cannot make a mistake, if only you are very attentive to notice every mark and the corresponding one on the next page, confiding in me that everything is right. Observe my spelling and punctuation very carefully, and never think you know better. I am the soul, you the body. Whatever is written in Latin characters, in square brackets, is meant as a notice for you alone. Wherever you see a line struck out, look carefully whether one word of it has remained standing, and let the last thing you ever think or believe be that I have been guilty of any negligence. Sometimes I have repeated in Roman letters on the margin, or between the lines, and enclosed in square brackets, a strange word that might be unfamiliar to you. If you find the numerous corrections tiresome, consider that just because of these I shall never need to improve my style on the proof-sheets, and thus give you double trouble.'

This new edition was issued in 1844 and attracted little attention. The fact that so powerful and original a work, one too that possessed the grand merit of lucidity, a merit almost unknown in the German philosophical world, should have fallen almost still-born from the press a second time, speaks most unfavourably for the independent judgment of the German public. Large allowance must, however, be made for the debased political state of the country : all intellectual interest and vigour were sapped ; such as existed found expression in patriotic conspiracies and enthusiasms : young Germany was too preoccupied, old Germany too apathetic, to probe a new system of philosophy. The storm was brewing, the horrors of the revolution were soon to burst, but Schopenhauer, absorbed in his speculations, had not felt the pulse of his age carefully enough to recognise that these hateful disturbances would prove the thunderstorm that clears the atmosphere of impurities and makes room for more vigorous life.

In 1846 Schopenhauer made the acquaintance of Julius Frauenstädt, who at once became his Metrodorus. Attracted by 'Die Welt als Wille und Vorstellung,' he sought an interview with the philosopher, the more readily accorded as he had preceded his visit by a laudatory notice of Schopenhauer's philosophy. He was even admitted at the unusual hour of eleven, when he found the philosopher lying on the sofa reading. Schopenhauer sprang up to meet his guest with cordiality, and Frauenstadt was charmed by his manner and appearance, so well in keeping with all he had anticipated. The leonine head revealed the powerful intellect and the mental work it had compassed ; though only fifty-eight, hair and beard were already snow-white, and harmonised with the idea of the sage, but the eyes flashed youthful fire, and the play of features was as lively as a boy's. A sarcastic line round the mouth alone revealed the misanthrope. Open and confiding as Schopenhauer was with those whom he saw reason to trust, he at once plunged *in medias res* with Frauenstadt, inveighing against the professors of philosophy who ignored his system and kept it out of repute. He then passed on to speak of a subject at that time largely occupying his thoughts.

'You will hardly guess,' he said, 'what book I was reading when you came in. It is one of the oldest dreambooks, the 'Oneirokritikon' of Artemidoros. For two years I have been studying somnambulism and ghostly apparitions for the sake of a metaphysical explanation of the same. It will only occupy a few pages in print, but to be able to write them I was obliged to examine the whole wide range of these phenomena, and consult ancient and modern literature on the subject. In fact no one would think from my discussions of the most important and difficult metaphysical problems, which only fill a few pages, by what enormous study they have been preceded. But this has always been my way ; I always intimately acquainted myself with the subject before I began to write about it. Thus for one whole winter I devoted myself entirely to ancient Greek tragedies, for the sake of the few pages about tragedy in the second volume of "Die Welt" : another time I studied thorough bass for my Metaphysics of Music, and so on.'

When Frauenstadt urged him to give explanations concerning clairvoyance and apparitions, he showed plainly he did not wish to anticipate his printed comments, but hinted that his solution of the problem was based on Kant's doctrine of the ideality of time and space. He willingly told stories bearing on this subject, and especially dwelt on one that had occurred to himself. All this he related in the graphic vivid manner peculiar to his speech, which made listening to his talk so rare a pleasure. The story is repeated in the 'Parerga,' under the title 'Versuch über das Geistersehen' :

'One morning I was very busy writing a long English business letter, of great importance to me ; when I had finished the third page I took up the ink instead of the sand and poured it out over the letter ; the ink flowed down from the desk on to the floor. The servant who came on my ringing the bell, fetched a, pail of water and washed the floor with it, so that the spots might not sink in. During this work she said to me : "I dreamt last night that I was washing inkstains out of the floor." Upon which I : "That is not true." She repeated : "It is true, and when I woke I told my fellow-servant who sleeps with me." Just then by chance the other servant, a girl of about seventeen, came in to call away the one who was scrubbing. I go towards her and say : "What did she dream last night? " Answer : "I don't know." Then I : "Yes, she told you when she woke." The young servant : "Oh yes, she dreamt that she would wash inkspots out of the floor." This story, for whose truth I can vouch, removes theorematic dreams beyond the range of doubt, and is not the less remarkable because what was dreamt was the result of an action which might be called involuntary, since I committed it quite without intention, and it depended upon a little slip of my hand : yet the action was so necessarily and inevitably determined beforehand that its result stood in the consciousness of another person several hours before it took place. Here the truth of my proposition Everything that happens happens of necessity, is evidently conspicuous.'

Interested as the disciple was in all these explanations, he desired above all to hear about Schopenhauer's main work ; but here the warning housekeeper appeared, and he was dismissed. After this he seems to have called so frequently that his receptions grew less cordial, Schopenhauer giving him to understand most plainly that he could not suffer such frequent interruptions. Relenting after a while, he fixed certain days and hours at which Frauenstadt might visit him. After this followed a weekly personal intercourse extending over five months, prized by

Frauenstadt as some of the richest and happiest hours of his life. Occasionally he was even privileged to accompany the philosopher on his promenades, the first of these being the memorable one under a melting July sun. When their personal intercourse was broken by Frauenstadt's removal from Frankfurt, it was carried on by correspondence, continued at intervals till within a year of Schopenhauer's death. It is a matter of dispute between Schopenhauer's disciples whether or no their master forbade them to publish his letters. The balance inclines to the side of non-publication, and internal evidence confirms the supposition. Schopenhauer was extremely careful in all he wrote that was intended for print ; he kept his best thoughts for his works, and if he ever uttered any in conversation or letters, he at once engrafted them into his notes for new editions. His letters, with these occasional exceptions, deal with ephemeral matters. Frauenstadt made him acquainted with all reviews and comments on his books ; Schopenhauer answered, criticised, abused, asked favours, acknowledged them, all with his own peculiar raciness ingrained. People still living are spoken of by name and not always in the most flattering terms. The letters are the unpremeditated effusions of friend to friend, not the accurately balanced words meant for the public eye. Their interest for the world is too limited to justify their publication. Schopenhauer would not have approved of his disciples' excess of zeal. For long weary years his life was an entrenchment against his enemies ; since his death he adds but another to the long list of great men whose weary echo from beyond the grave would be, Defend me from my friends!

The mutterings of the approaching thunderstorm grew louder and more ominous. Schopenhauer was not easily roused by political disturbances, but when they interfered with his peace of mind he could no longer ignore them. The serious riots in September 1847 first excited his uneasiness, and his old fears of ill once more came over him with increased strength. It was impossible to foresee what might result from the general confusion : Schopenhauer trembled at the thought of King Mob's rule. Such political views as he had were expressed in his firm conviction of the necessity of a monarchy. 'A King should say, instead of "we by the grace of God," "we the least of two evils." The election of Archduke John as Regent of the Empire temporarily allayed his disquietude, but not sufficiently to prevent him from curtailing his expenses and remanding some book orders. He writes in June, 1848 : —

'My health is the same as usual, and I suppose posterity will probably have to wait before the door awhile. But I have had terrible mental suffering these last four months through anxiety and worry. All property and civil conditions were threatened; at my age one is much affected by these things, when the staff that has supported one through life, and of which one has shown oneself worthy, begins to fail. Well, *inde salus, unde origo* (supply—*malorum*). Thirty years ago I read this on a gravestone at Venice. The Parisians sowed the seed, and have reaped it ; they drew us into the mire, and, *si Diis placet*, will pull us out again. Not more than fair.'

Schopenhauer's resemblance to Goethe in all that concerns politics is certainly striking ; both hated violent revolutions because they check intellectual development and result in retrogression of culture. The people he held to be a sovereign eternally a minor, who must therefore remain under constant guardianship, and can never manage his own affairs without causing endless troubles. The August riots reawakened his alarm ; the cowardly murder of Prince Felix Lichnowsky and General von Auerswald heightened it to frenzy ; in his fear of democratic rule he was almost resolved to fly the city. This dastardly deed embittered his contempt for the insurgents and for the phraseology so current of 'liberty,' 'happiness,' and 'freedom of the people,' which he held as hollow twaddle. He was at that time busy on the 'Parerga and Paralipomena,' a philosophical work that may claim the adjective charming one— truly not often applied to works of this class. He wrote to Frauenstädt :

Frankfort, March 2, 1849.

'My opera mixta are constantly in hand, but my maxim is *sat cito sat bene*; I do not expect to have finished till the end of this year, and by the next, *Diis et bibliopolis volentibus*, they are to appear. They will be voluminous, so that one volume will scarcely contain them, and they must be made into two. Then I will wipe my pen and say "the rest is silence." But in case I should die before that, I hereby empower you to claim and edit the MS. and draw the profit, for when once I am dead, my writings will be worth money, scarcely before. But I suppose nothing will come of it ; with my imperturbable health and strength I shall live to see many another bad year. Every thing is as usual with me ; Atma sends his love. But what have we gone through! Imagine on the 18th of September there was a barricade on the bridge and the scoundrels stood close to my house, aiming and shooting at the soldiers in the street, whose return shots shook the house. Suddenly voices and knocking at the locked door of my room ; I, thinking it to be the sovereign *canaille*, bar the door, then follow dangerous thumpings ; at last the soft voice of my servant : "It is only a few Austrians." I immediately open to these dear friends ; twenty blue-trousered Bohemians rush in to shoot from my window upon the mobility, but soon they think they can do it better from the next house. From the first floor the officer surveys the rabble behind the barricade, I immediately send him the large double opera glass through which you once saw the balloon, and Ψυχων σοΦων τοντ ἐστί Φροντιστήριον. (Aristoph. Nubes.)

At last peace was enforced, though differences were not adjusted, and dissension and discontent still existed. The nation forcibly reduced to submission was dispirited and broken. Schopenhauer did not recognise at once how fatal the year 1848 had been to Hegelianism. The bitter experience of the revolution was followed by despair ; the time was ripe when a preacher of despair would find eager listeners. But he was working on steadily at the book that should at last open all eyes to him. Meanwhile the new edition of 'Die Welt als Wille und Vorstellung' was slowly making way, and disciples occasionally turned up in Frankfort, lured thither in the hope of seeing face to face the writer who had attracted them so powerfully.

'There arises a silent congregation, which I had rather were a noisy one. . . . No abuse is too bad for servants who are enemies of the master whose bread they eat, and this is the relation of its professors to philosophy.'

All this was intensely grateful to Schopenhauer, and he does not fail to record every such occurrence. At the end of 1849 he writes :

'Everything is as usual with me. I am busy writing at the opera mixta, which will be ready for press in the spring. Then we will consider about a publisher. I have lost my dear, precious, large, beautiful poodle ; he died of old age, not quite ten years old. It has grieved me sincerely and long.'

In September 1850 he could say to Frauenstädt :

'My opera mixta are finished, after six years daily work, now it is *manum de tabula!* and—I cannot find a publisher. . . . The circumstance is vexatious, but not humiliating ; for the papers announce that Lola Montes intends to write her memoirs, and English publishers have immediately offered her large sums. So we know what we are about. But I really do not know what more I can do, and whether my opera mixta are not destined to be posthumous, when there will be no want of publishers. Meanwhile, I am really writing to-day to ask if you, my true Theophrastus and Metrodorus, will try to hunt up a publisher for me among the many booksellers in Berlin. In case you should be able to do this, I enclose the table of contents. This alone suffices to show that this book is far more suitable for general readers than any of my former ones, and might thus more easily find a publisher. I might almost call it, from the greater part of its contents, my "Philosopher for the World." I only make the condition that a decent German, not Roman type, should be used, not smaller nor closer than that of my 2nd edition, and that every sheet shall be sent me for correction, which is indispensable . . . . If you should be successful, you would have done a true service to me and to philosophy. I have always refused to publish on my own account, and to be posthumous, it would have to wait some time, for my health is excellent, and I am still as active as when I dragged you a walk that night mid snow and wind.'

Dr. Frauenstädt's endeavours were successful after many failures, and Schopenhauer was deeply grateful.

Frankfort, September 30, 1850.

'MY DEAR DR. FRAUENSTÄDT,
'You are a real true friend and *optime meritus de nobis et philosophia nostra* in every way. My sincerest thanks for your trouble and zeal in procuring a publisher. I hope the man will not do badly for himself, for much of it, especially the Aphorisms for the Conduct of Life, which occupy half the first volume, are very popular in style. But it is the fault of the times that it is so difficult to find publishers for such books. Everyone is up to the ears in politics. If for any reason the publisher wished to begin the printing somewhat later, instead of leaving the MS. with him, I would rather keep it here, because it might occur to me to alter or add something. I part unwillingly from this, my last work, for " the rest is silence." .... Read the conditions of the contract to Hayn in a stentorian voice. I will not swerve from them. I ask little enough for a six years' daily (two first morning hours') work, the preparations for which have extended over thirty years of my life, for things like mine cannot be shaken out of one's sleeve. For where, in the range of German literature, is there another book which, wherever it is opened, immediately reveals more thoughts than it is possible to grasp, like my second volume of " Die Welt als Wille und Vorstellung." (For shame, old man, don't blow your own trumpet!) Finally, the publisher must promise to add to the announcement of my book no praise, recommendation or other comment ; on the other hand he can, if he likes, print the table of contents.'

CHAPTER X - HIS ETHICS AND AESTHETICS

SCHOPENHAUER'S ethics are implied in the leading principle of his system. Everything hinges upon the affirmation or negation of 'the Will to live.' When this is affirmed, *i.e.* when the individual's actions are directly or indirectly controlled by the wish to possess, enjoy, perpetuate, or embellish existence, 'the imaginations of the heart are corrupt and evil continually.' In proportion as individuality loses its value for the individual, as he recognises that it is in fact an illusion and that he exists in others as much as in himself, he advances along the path of virtue. For, as Schopenhauer justly remarks, the greatest criminals are the greatest egotists. All wrong doing is in the last analysis resolvable into contempt for the rights of others, into pursuit of one's own advantage, in affirmation of 'the Will to live' at their expense. In its coarsest form this implies the commission of crimes of violence punishable by the legislator, but between these and the most refined forms of egotism the difference is merely one of degree. Right moral action can spring only from the recognition of the essential evil of the phenomenal world, and the deliberate resolve to reduce it to a minimum. The secret of this lies in one word, abnegation. 'The Will to live' comprehends self-assertion in every form and shape, and as every charitable action involves the denial of self in some respect, it follows that Schopenhauer's morality is in the main equivalent to the inculcation of universal philanthropy. He thus may appear at one with those optimistic moralists of whom Franklin may be regarded as the type ; but starting from such opposite premises he cannot but arrive at dissimilar conclusions. He begins where Franklin ends. According to the latter no type of human excellence can be higher than that of the exemplary citizen. Schopenhauer also commends the patriot, but from a transcendental motive which Franklin would have been wholly unable to comprehend.

'The man who dies for his country has freed himself from the delusion that existence is limited to his individual person ; he expands his own being over that of his fellow countrymen, through whom he continues to live. He even extends it over coming generations, for whom also he labours. He regards death as the blinking of an eyelid, which does not interrupt sight.'

In Schopenhauer's eyes *he* is the patriot who has, for the time, emancipated himself from the conception of the substantial existence of his individual being ; for whom it is entirely obliterated in the more liberal idea of country ; for whom, accordingly, it is for the moment a mere delusion. Let this conception be applied to all human relations, and action, conformable to the laws of morality, will inevitably result. The individual will lose the conception of his individuality ; he will no longer regard himself as a real existence, comprised within the rigid line of personality, and thus insulated and differentiated from the rest of the universe. He will regard his separate being as a mere transitory phenomenon, a temporary objectivation of the sole real existence, and this recognition of his true position must necessarily destroy selfishness, which proceeds on the assumption of such an actual distinction between individuals as to allow of the genuine, not the merely illusive, transfer of advantage from one side to the other. The wisdom of the sage, therefore, should easily pass from theory into practice.

'Wisdom is not merely theoretical, but also practical perfection ; it is the ultimate true cognition of all things in mass and in detail, which has so penetrated man's being that it appears as the guide of all his actions. The wisdom that imbues a man with mere theory not developed into practice, resembles the double rose, which pleases by its colour and fragrance, but drops, leaving no fruit.'

The artist attains the same result by a somewhat different path.

'At such times as we are exalted by the power of intellect, and relinquish the usual manner of regarding things, that mere investigation of their relations to each other, whose final end is always their relation to our own will, then we no longer regard the Where, When, Whence and Wherefore of things, but only the What. At such times we are not occupied by abstract thought, the conceptions of reason and consciousness, but instead of these the whole power of our intellect is devoted to contemplation, is entirely absorbed in it, and the consciousness is filled by the quiet contemplation of the natural object before us, whether a landscape, a tree, a rock, a building, or whatever it may be. To use a significant expression, it (the consciousness) is lost in the object, that is, forgets its individuality, its Will, and remains a mere subject, a clear mirror to the object. It is then as though the object alone existed without any one to contemplate it, and it is no longer possible to distinguish the contemplator from the thing contemplated. Both are merged into one, for the whole consciousness is occupied by a single perceptible picture. When the object has thus lost all relation to everything outside itself, and the subject has retired from all its relations to the Will, then what is recognised is no longer the single thing as such, but the Idea, the Eternal Form, and therefore he who is absorbed in this contemplation is no longer an individual, for the individual has lost himself in this contemplation; he is merely the subject of cognition, knowing neither will, pain, nor time. In such contemplation the single thing becomes at one stroke the Idea of its species, and the perceiving individual the pure subject of cognition.'

Far before the artist, however, is the ascetic ; he who has fairly recognised the Will to live as the source of all evil, and has resolved to destroy it by persistent mortification.

'When a man ceases to draw an egotistic distinction between himself and others, and takes as much part in their sorrows as in his own, it naturally follows that such an one, recognising his own self in all beings, must regard the endless griefs of all living as his own, and thus appropriate to himself the sorrows of the whole world. He apprehends the whole, seizes its being, acknowledges the nullity of all struggle, and his cognition becomes the quietus of Will. Will now turns away from life, man attains to the state of voluntary renunciation, to resignation, to negation of the will to live. The phenomenon by which this is shown, the aversion to the world, to the Will to live, is the transition from virtue to asceticism.'

This is the great saving truth, the *quod semper, quod ubique, quod ab omnibus*.

'In reading the lives of Christian and Indian peni- tents, we are greatly struck by their similarity. With an utter dissimilarity of dogmas, customs, and external circumstances, their aspirations and inner life are identical. . . . . . Quietism, *i.e.*, renunciation of all Will ; asceticism, *i.e.*, voluntary stifling of self-will ; and mysticism, *i.e.*, the recognition of the identity of the individual with the All, or the core of the universe : these all stand in close connection, so that he who acknowledges one of them is gradually led to take up the others, even against his intention. Nothing is more astonishing than the unanimity of all who profess these principles, notwithstanding the greatest diversity of age, country and religion. They do not form a sect, indeed they are mostly ignorant of each other's existence. The Indian, Christian, and Mahommedan mystics, quietists, and ascetics are disparate in all things, only not in the inner spirit and meaning of their teachings. . . . So much concord among such divergent peoples and times is a practical proof that theirs is not a distorted and perverted state of mind, but the expression of an essential constituent of human nature, whose rarity is due solely to its excellence.'

It will be at once apparent that in its practical ethical aspect Schopenhauer's teaching differs in nothing from Buddhism. The reference of all existence to egotistic desire, the conclusion that as such it must be essentially evil, the further corollary that the road to the extinction of sorrow can only lie through the extinction of desire, and that this can only be attained by the mortification of every passion ; these are the very commonplaces of Buddhistic teaching. The spirit in which they are urged is indeed very different. No two things can be much more dissimilar than Schopenhauer's angry invective and Buddha's mild persuasiveness; nor perhaps is the whole body of his ethical doctrine so expressive as Buddha's matchless definition of virtue : 'The agreement of the Will with the Conscience.' Substantially, however, the accordance is perfect ; and there can be no doubt that Schopenhauer's philosophy is but one symptom among many of the modification which European thought is at present undergoing from the influx of Oriental ideas. Schopenhauer is fully conscious of his coincidence with Buddhism, which he prefers to Brahminism on account of its more complete freedom from mythology and its finding the way to blessedness rather by inward mortification, charity and humility than by painful or disgusting penance. At the same time, as will be inferred from the last quotation, he maintains that the spirit of true religion is everywhere the same; he speaks with the greatest respect of Christianity, apart from what he deems its mythology, asserting that the spirit of the New Testament is wholly on his side.

The assumption of the sorrows of humanity ascribed by Christianity to the condescension of a supernatural person, is, according to Schopenhauer, imposed upon every man by the mere fact of his having been born into the world—happy he who recognises and fulfils his duty! The religions which assume the reality of this phenomenal universe, or promise their followers earthly bliss as the reward of obedience to their precepts, are Schopenhauer's especial abomination. Like the early Gnostics he insists on the absolute irreconcilability of Christianity with the Judaism on which it has been grafted, he maintains this latter to be merely the Persian religion in a slightly modified form.

'Christianity is composed of two heterogeneous ingredients ; an ethical view of life akin to Hindooism and a Jewish dogma. Its ethics are crippled by this latter foreign element, and cannot attain definite expression. The purely ethical element must be considered as pre-eminently, nay, exclusively Christian, distinct from the Jewish dogmatism to which it was unnaturally united. . . .'

'The theory of the redemption of mankind and of the world is evidently of Indian origin, and presupposes the Indian religion, which teaches that creation itself (that Sansara of the Buddhists), is the work of evil. This had to be engrafted by Christianity on Jewish theism, according to which not only did God make the world, but afterwards deemed it very good. Thence the difficulties and contradictions in the Christian doctrine, and that strange guise of the Christian mysteries which is so distasteful to common sense. . . . '

'In truth the spirit and ethical tendency of Christianity are closely connected with Brahminism and Buddhism and not with the Judaic πάντα καλὰ λίαν ('behold it was very good,' Gen. i. 31). The essence of a religion consists in its spirit and ethical tendency, and not in the myths in which they are clothed. In its ethical teachings Christianity points to these ancient religions as the source whence it sprang. By virtue of this origin (or at least of this concord) Christianity belongs to the old true sublime belief of humanity, as opposed to the false, ignoble, noxious optimism embodied in Greek heathenism, in Judaism, and in Islam.'

'Christian morality, but for the defect of ignoring the animal world, would manifest the utmost similarity to that of Brahminism and Buddhism, and is only less emphatically expressed and deficient in logical consistency. We can therefore hardly doubt that this, as well as the idea of a god becoming man (Avatar), originated in India, and came to Judea by way of Egypt, so that

Christianity is a reflection of old Indian light from the ruins of Egypt, which unfortunately fell upon Jewish ground.'

Schopenhauer's censure comprehends not only the narrow and restrictive spirit of Mosaism, but also the cheerful creed of Greece. There can be no question that his doctrine is virtually identical with that of Christian, no less than of Buddhist saints, and contains as many elements of truth. Whether Greece could ever have become what she was under such a system of thought; whether, logically carried out, it is not destructive of all culture, and inimical to every advance in national prosperity; whether it would not reduce the people embracing it to Indian apathy and quietism; are questions which it behoves those fascinated by its many beauties carefully to consider.

In one respect Schopenhauer's ethical system appears at a disadvantage when compared with Buddha's : the slight stress laid upon right action as a means of obtaining deliverance from suffering. According to the Buddhist sages, charitable deeds possess almost equal value with the perception of truth, and moral demerit is among the most potent causes of the detention of mortals in the world of phenomena. With Schopenhauer the intellectual conditions of salvation are more powerfully accentuated than the moral ; it may be questioned whether his instructions would ever have produced 'the enthusiasm of humanity ' which found such powerful expression in the edicts of King Asoka. To select a minor point for illustration's sake : the distinction is strikingly apparent in one of the precepts in which his coincidence with Buddha is most marked, the inculcation of kindness to animals. With Buddha this seems to repose simply upon the instinct of compassion. Schopenhauer gives it a philosophical basis ; with him animals are imperfect men, incarnations of the universal Will in a more primitive form ; their kinship to mankind is no mere figure of speech, but the simplest and most literal matter of fact. It is needless to point out how thoroughly Schopenhauer's views on this head are borne out by the Darwinian theory. It may be added that should the human race be shown to have sprung from more than one progenitor, they will constitute the only ground on which, apart from natural human feeling, it will be possible to maintain the rights of the inferior races of mankind. This precept is, not withstanding, dependent to a great degree upon philosophical theory. The animal world is also especially interesting to him, as exhibiting the irrationality of the will to live, i.e. of the phenomenal universe in its naked deformity.

'To regard the overruling desire of all animals and human beings to preserve and continue life as long as possible, as original and absolute, it is necessary that we should clearly understand that it is in no manner the result of an objective acknowledgment of the value of life, but is independent of all cognition, or in other words, that these beings are not drawn, but driven.'

'For this purpose, let us contemplate the countless series of animals, their endless variety of form modified according to element and mode of life, and at the same time consider the inimitable ingenuity of their construction and function equally developed in each species, and finally the incredible expenditure of power, skill, prudence, and activity, which every animal has to make in the course of its life. Examining the matter more closely, observe the restless industry of little wretched ants, the wonderful and skilful perseverance of the bees, or watch a single burying beetle (Necrophorus Vespillo) bury a mole forty times its own size in two days, in which to deposit its eggs, and insure nourishment for its future brood. This shows us how in reality the life of most insects is nothing but an endless labour to prepare food and dwelling for the brood which is to spring from their eggs, and which when they have devoured the nutriment, and become chrysalises, only enter into life to repeat the same operations. Similarly, the life of birds is almost spent in their far and weary wanderings, in the building of their nests, and in fetching food for the brood, who, next year, will enact the same part. Everything thus works for the future, which proves as bankrupt as the present. When we consider all this, we cannot help looking around for the reward of all this skill and trouble, for the end which makes these creatures strive so restlessly, and ask ourselves : What is the aim of all this ? what is attained by this animal existence, which requires such immeasurable exertions ? The only answer is : The satisfaction of hunger and the propagation of the species, and at best a little momentary pleasure such as now and then falls to the lot of every animal individual between his eternal needs and exertions. If we compare the indescribable skill of preparation, the inexhaustible riches of the means, and the insignificance of the end in view,, the conviction is forced upon us that life is a business whose profits do not nearly cover its expenses.'

In the blind yet efficacious instinct of animals, more especially of insects, Schopenhauer discerns the clearest proof and illustration of the unconscious action of that impulse to which he ascribes the origination of the universe. It is only at an advanced stage of the world-constructing process that intelligence supervenes, involving the possibility of moral responsibility. The question of the freedom of the Will, and con- sequent merit or demerit, is as great a perplexity to him as to all other philosophers. Not that he has the smallest hesitation in rejecting the ordinary view on this subject as an absurd figment ; his arguments on this head, like those of other necessarian philosophers, are logically impregnable, but he has made no progress towards finding a place for moral approbation and dis- approbation. The sum of his doctrines is that free action consists not in *operari* but in *esse* ; that man is free in so far as his existence is a reality, as he exists beyond the limits of time, space, and other mere forms of perception, but that he is subject to the most stringent necessity as a phenomenal being. Unfortunately it is in this light alone that moralists and magistrates have anything to do with him, and we must feel that Schopenhauer has in no way aided us to bridge over the gulf between theory and practice. His great originality consists in his powerful assertion, contrary to the ordinary opinion, of the vast predominance of the instinctive element of human nature (the Will, in his vocabulary) over the reflective (the Intellect).

'Intellect flags, Will is indefatigable. After continuous headwork, the brain is fatigued, like the arm after continuous bodily labour. All cognition is connected with exertion, but to will is our individual being, whose manifestations continue without any trouble and entirely of themselves. Therefore, when the Will is greatly excited, as in all passions—in anger, fear, desire, sorrow, &c.—and we are summoned to understand the motives of these passions in order to rectify them, the compulsion we have to exert over ourselves attests the transition from the original, natural, and individual activity, to that which is derived, indirect and constrained. Will alone is uninvited, therefore often too ready and too strong in its activity, knowing no fatigue. Infants, who scarcely manifest the first faint traces of intelligence, are already full of self-will. By purposeless kicking and crying they show the power of will with which they are overflowing, although their will has as yet no object, *i.e.*, they will, without knowing what they will. Precipitation, a fault which is more or less common to all men, and is only conquered by education, is another proof of the indefatigable energy of the will. It consists in the will hurrying before its time to the work. Being a purely active and executive function, it should not assert itself until the explorative and deliberative, and therefore the apprehending power, has entirely completed its task. But this moment is rarely awaited. Scarcely have we seized and hastily connected by cognition a few data on the circumstances in question—a particular event, or an opinion expressed by another— than out of the depth of our being there arises, uninvited, the ever-ready, never-tiring Will, and manifests itself as terror, fear, hope, pleasure, desire, envy, sorrow, zeal, anger, courage ; and impels to rash words and deeds. These are generally followed by remorse, when time has taught us that the hegemon, the intellect, was not half able to finish its work of understanding the circumstances, considering their relation, and determining what should be done, because the will would wait no longer, and sprang up long before its time with : Now it is my turn. . . . Of ten things that vex us, nine would not have the power to do so if we understood them and their causes thoroughly, and therefore recognised their necessity and true condition. We should do this much oftener if we made them sooner an object of consideration, and not of rashness, and vexation. For the intellect is to the will in man what the bridle and bit are to an untamed horse : it must be led by this bridle, by means of instruction, warning, education, &c., or alone it is as wild and fierce an impulse as the power shown in the dashing waterfall, and is, as we know, in its root identical with it. In the most violent anger, in despair, in intoxication, it has taken the bit between its teeth, has run away and followed its original nature. In the *mania sine delirio* it has lost bit and bridle, and plainly shows its original nature, and that the intellect is as foreign to it as the bridle to the horse. In this state it may be compared to a watch which runs down unchecked when deprived of a certain screw.'

It will be easily apprehended that the passion of love, and everything relating to the perpetuation of the species, must necessarily attract the special attention of Schopenhauer. The phenomenal world being the realisation of the eternal Will to live, the sexual instinct is, as respects the intelligent portion of it, the. machinery employed by the will to accomplish this end. The aim of Nature merely regards the perpetuation of the species ; the individual is as nothing to her. While seeming to act for himself, in reality he is impelled by the force of which he is the manifestation in time, and which aims at perpetuating itself through his action. The poetry of love is mainly illusion and glittering drapery, designed to mantle the stern solemnity of the thing as it really is. If man perceived this, if he had acuteness to unmask the delusion of instinct, and strength to withstand the torrent of desire, he might, by simply refusing to become an accomplice in the design of Nature, bring the whole tragedy of existence to an end.

'All love, however ethereally it comports itself, is rooted solely in desire ; indeed, is really but a certain, specified, individual sexual inclination. Let us in this sense regard the important part played by this passion in all its modifications and shades, not only in dramas and novels, but in real life, where, next to love of life, it is the most powerful spring of action. It ceaselessly occupies the strength and thought of the younger portion of mankind, is the final goal of all human endeavours, exerts a noxious influence over the most important concerns, interrupts at any hour the most serious occupations, confuses for a time even the most vigorous intellects, does not hesitate to interpose its frivolity amid the conferences of statesmen and the researches of scholars, places its love-letters and locks of hair between ministerial portfolios and philosophic manuscripts, daily knits the worst and most entangled *liaisons*, loosens the most sacred relationships, the firmest ties ; causes the sacrifice of rank, happiness, and even wealth ; makes the honourable man unscrupulous, the faithful man a traitor : in short, appears everywhere as an antagonistic demon that turns all things upside down. When we regard all this, we are forced to exclaim : Why all this fuss? why all this striving and rushing, this trouble and anxiety? The upshot is merely that every Jack finds his Jill ; why should such a trifle play so important a part, and bring incessant interruption and confusion into the life of men? To the serious inquirer the spirit of truth slowly reveals the answer. It is no trifle that is here agitated ; the importance of the subject is worthy the serious zeal of these practices. The aim of all these love affairs, whether played in sock or buskin, is really more important than all the other aims in man's life, and therefore worthy the deep earnestness with which each pursues it ; for that which is decided by it is nothing less than the composition of the next generation. The existence and quality of the *dramatis personae* who shall appear on the boards, when we have stepped off them, is decided by these so frivolous love affairs.'

The perpetuation of species being thus the sole real end of the passion of love, no surprise need be felt at the constant disappointment of expectations of ideal bliss, which are in fact but portions of a machinery instituted for the working out of quite another purpose. Nature has already attained the sole end which she proposed to herself.

'Love marriages are contracted in the interest of the species, not of the individuals. It is true that those most concerned fancy they are promoting their own happiness; still their true aim is one foreign to themselves, and must be sought in the creation of an individual possible only to them. United for this purpose, they should endeavour to get on together as well as possible ; but very often a pair united by this instinctive delusion is otherwise most heterogeneous. This appears when delusion vanishes, as it necessarily must ; therefore love marriages generally prove unhappy. Thanks to them, the coming generation is provided for at the cost of the present. *Quien se casa por amores, ha de vivir con dolores*, says the Spanish proverb (Who marries for love, lives with sorrow). The reverse holds good with marriages contracted for convenience, mostly by choice of the parents. The considerations that determine these marriages are real, and do not vanish of themselves. By them present happiness is postponed to the future, which after all is problematical. A man who considers money instead of the satisfaction of affection, lives more for the individual than for the species. This is opposed to truth, and is consequently unnatural, and calls forth contempt. A girl who, contrary to her parents' advice, refuses a rich man not too advanced in years, and who, disregarding considerations of prudence, chooses according to her instinctive liking, sacrifices her individual well-being to the species. On this account one cannot withhold from her a certain admiration ; she has chosen the more important, and acted according to the sense of nature (more accurately, the species), while her parents counsel her in the sense of individual egotism. From all this it will appear that marriage can seldom be contracted but at the expense of either the species or the individual. This is generally the case ; for convenience and passionate love to go hand in hand is the rarest piece of good fortune. The miserable physical, moral, or intellectual constitution of most men may be partly the cause why marriages are not usually contracted from free choice and affection, but from convenience and accidental circumstances. If, however, affection is somewhat regarded together with convenience, this is a sort of compromise with the species. Happy marriages are proverbially rare, just because it is the essence of marriage that its object should be not the present but the coming generation. Meanwhile, for the comfort of tender loving hearts, it may be added, that passionate sexual love is occasionally united to real friendship, based upon uniformity of sentiment, though this generally appears only when passion is extinguished by gratification.'

Prosaic as may appear this reference of the most ideal of human passions to a simply utilitarian end, Love, in Schopenhauer's conception, nevertheless amply merits the radiance with which Poetry has invested it. First, on account of the vast importance of the matter, compared with which all other forms of human activity sink into insignificance, inasmuch as it is the essential condition and indispensable foundation of them all ; secondly, for a reason peculiarly characteristic of Schopenhauer.

'The yearning of love (ἱμερος), which has been sung in endless variety by the poets of all ages without exhausting the subject, nay, without ever doing it justice ; the yearning which connects with the possession of a particular woman the ideal of eternal bliss, and inexpressible pain at the thought that it is not to be attained ; this yearning, and this pain of love, cannot take their substance from the needs of an ephemeral individual, but they are the sighs of the spirit of species, which here sees a never-to-be-recovered means of gaining or losing its ends, and therefore emits this groan. The species alone has endless life, and is therefore capable of endless wishes, endless satisfaction, and endless pain. But these are pent within the narrow breast of a mortal ; no wonder, then, if it seems to burst, and can find no expression for the all-pervading presentiment of endless joy or sorrow. This therefore furnishes material for all the finest erotic poetry, which rises accordingly into transcendental metaphors surpassing everything earthly. This is the theme of Petrarch, the material for a St. Preux, a Werther, and a Jacopo Ortis, which could otherwise be neither explained nor understood.'

Schopenhauer's speculations on Love form one of the most original and brilliant chapters of his writings. If at first they appear harshly prosaic and almost repulsive, this will be found on examination to arise rather from the idiosyncrasy of the author than the intrinsic nature of the theory. Nearly the same view of the purpose subserved by passion in the general economy of things will be found in the concluding passages of Emerson's beautiful essay 'On Love.' The comparison of the two strikingly illustrates the contrast which the same opinions may be made to represent accordingly as they have passed through the medium and imbibed the hues of a morose and disdainful or of a cheerful and affectionate spirit. It further results, that while Schopenhauer and Emerson are agreed in regarding love (which to the lover is both end and means), as merely a means towards an end, the scaffolding as it were of the human edifice, they differ completely in their estimate of the position of woman. Schopenhauer, recognising the strength of instinct and keenness of intuition in the female sex, sees in it a closer manifestation of the original cause of being. Woman is but one remove from 'the will to live.' Man has advanced a step into intelligence, and is so far nearer to emancipation. ['When Nature divided humanity into male and female, her section was not precisely a bisection. The distinction of the positive and negative poles is not merely qualitative but quantitative also.'] Woman is entitled to indulgence, but to claim deference for her is ridiculous. The Greek and Oriental treatment of the sex was much more rational than that which obtains in Modern Europe, where, if the *ladies* are pampered, the *women* are worse off than elsewhere. Mingled with this misogyny are acute and profound remarks on the undeniably weak points in the female character, such as women's habitual disregard of abstract justice, and lack of consideration for inferiors. It will be remembered that Schopenhauer, so far as we know, was an utter stranger to intimacy with intellectual or distinguished women, that he seems never to have met one capable of reflecting his ideas. Had this been the case, he might not have so roundly denied the very possibility of genius to women, even though the reason assigned, 'because they are wholly subjective,' is fully in harmony with the tenor of his philosophy.

Schopenhauer attributes to the artist, the man of genius, a perfection second only to that of the ascetic who has attained entire negation of the will. The reason is that he accomplishes, though only in moments of ecstasy, the same end of self-annihilation which the other habitually achieves. All art depends upon the apprehension of eternal ideas, intermediate between the phenomenal world and the world of essential reality. In aesthetic contemplation, the single object contemplated becomes the idea of its species, and the contemplating individual a pure organ of intelligence. The contemplator's personality is thus for the time abolished; he is swallowed up in the object, and so identified with it as to regard it as an accident of his own being. The veil of Maya is rent; the spectator is no longer under the illusion that hinders him from recognising himself in all other existence. Without this there may be talent but not genius; for genius, from one point of view, is the capacity for apprehending things as they actually are.

'Genius is objectivity. The more clearly and objectively things reveal themselves by contemplation (this fundamental and richest form of comprehension), the more they are really momentarily opposed in inverse ratio to the interest that the will takes in these same objects. Cognisance, freed from will, is the necessary condition, ay, the essence of all aesthetic comprehension. Why does an ordinary painter render a landscape so badly, notwithstanding all his pains? Because he does not see more beauty in it. And why does he not see more beauty in it? Because his intellect is not sufficiently separated from his will. The degrees of this separation mark great intellectual differences between men. Cognisance is the purer, and consequently the more objective and correct, the more it has freed itself from the will, as the fruit is best that has no taste of the soil on which it has grown.'

On the other hand:

'In reality, all bunglers are such because their intellect is too firmly bound up with their will, acts by its spur, and thus remains entirely in its service. Bunglers are therefore only capable of attaining personal ends; in accordance with these, they produce bad pictures, mindless poems, shallow, absurd, ay, even dishonest philosophies, if their object be to commend themselves to their dishonest superiors. All their doings and actions are personal. Therefore they merely endeavour to assume the fashion of true work—its exterior, accidental and attractive form—seizing the shell instead of the kernel, but fancying meanwhile that they have rivalled, ay, even surpassed, their models.'

It follows that works of talent exist for the sake of some end external to art, but works of genius for themselves.

'Just because genius consists in the free service of the intellect, emancipated from the service of the Will, its productions can serve no useful purposes, whether music, philosophy, painting or poetry: a work of genius is not a thing of utility. To be useless, belongs to the character of works of genius; it is their patent of nobility. All other human works exist for the maintenance or convenience of existence, only not those in question. They alone exist for themselves, and are in this sense to be regarded as the blossom, the real produce of existence. Therefore, in enjoying them, our hearts expand, for we rise above the heavy earthy atmosphere of needs. Thus we seldom see the beautiful and the useful combined : fine lofty trees bear no fruit ; fruit-trees are ugly little cripples ; the double garden rose is barren—only the little wild, scentless one is fruitful. The finest buildings are not the most useful ; a temple is no dwelling-house. A man endowed with rare intellectual gifts, who is forced to follow a merely useful profession which the most ordinary person might pursue, is like a costly painted vase used as a cooking utensil. To compare useful people to geniuses is like comparing bricks to diamonds.'

With all this the man of genius is not happy, for he is, in a certain sense, unnatural. Genius is an intelligence, which has revolted against its natural mission, the service of the will ; hence a long train of miseries and an habitual melancholy, resting mainly on this principle, that the clearer and brighter the intelligence that illuminates the Will, the more distinctly does the latter appreciate the misery of its condition. Yet the ecstasy of the man of genius affords while it lasts the perfect counterpart of the bliss which springs from absolute self-renunciation, and the entire dissipation of the illusion which persuades man of his individuality.

'We know that our happiest moments are those when (by aesthetic contemplation) we are freed from the fierce impulse of Will, and rise as it were above the heavy atmosphere of earth. From this we may infer how blessed must be the life of a man whose will is subdued for ever ; not at rare intervals, as in the enjoyment of the beautiful, but extinguished, except that last glimmering spark which sustains the body and will perish with it. Such a man, who has after many bitter combats conquered his own nature, remains only as a purely intellectual being—an untarnished mirror of the universe. Nothing has power to disturb or agitate him, for he has severed all the thousand threads of the Will, which bind us to the world and draw us hither and thither in constant pain, under the form of desire, fear, envy, anger. He can now look back calm and smiling on the juggleries of this world, which were once able to move and even disturb his mind. Now they stand as indifferently before him as the chessmen after the game is played out, or like discarded masks, that mocked and disquieted us during the Carnival. Life and its figures only pass before him like a fleeting apparition, a morning dream before one who is half awake ; reality shimmers through—it can no longer deceive, and like such a dream without abrupt transition they disappear at last.'

The general scope of Schopenhauer's system on the ethical side is contained in the following quotation from his great ethical essay :

'Every individual is a being naturally different from every other. In my own person I have my true being; everything else, on the other hand, is not I, and foreign to me.' This is the confession to which flesh and blood bear witness, which is at the root of all egotism, and whose practical expression is found in every loveless, unjust, or unkind action.

'My true inner being exists in every living creature as immediately as in my own consciousness it is made known to me. It is this confession, for which the Sanskrit formula is *tat-twam-asi*, i.e., this is yourself, that breaks forth as pity, on which every true, that is unselfish, virtue rests, and whose practical expression is every good deed. It is, finally, this conviction to which every appeal to gentleness, human love, and mercy is directed ; for these remind us of the respect in which we are all one and the same being. But egotism, envy, hatred, persecution, austerity, revenge, malice, cruelty, appeal to the former conviction, and are satisfied by it. The emotion and pleasure which we feel on hearing of, still more on seeing, but most of all on performing a noble action, spring from the certainty it gives us that beyond the multiplicity and variety of individuals there lies a unity which really exists and is accessible, since it has just actually shown itself.'

'The preponderance of one or the other of these modes of perception is discerned not only in single actions but in the whole mode of consciousness and disposition, which is therefore entirely different in a good character and in a bad one. The latter everywhere feels a rigid barrier between itself and everything outside it ; the world is an absolute 'Not I,' and its relation to it an originally hostile one. The keynote of its disposition is hatred, suspicion, envy, malice. On the other hand, a good character lives in an outer world homogeneous to his own being—all others are to him, instead of "Not I," "Myself once again;" therefore his relation to everyone is amicable : he feels himself inwardly akin to all, takes a direct interest in everyone's weal and woe, and confidently reckons upon the same sympathy from them. Hence the deep peace of his inner being, and that calm, confident, contented disposition which makes everyone happy in his presence.'

The above quotations have been principally derived from Schopenhauer's capital work on the Universe considered as a Manifestation of Will. This is a great book in more senses than one. Goethe seems to have been unable to get to the end of it. General readers may study Schopenhauer with more advantage in the two volumes of minor essays entitled 'Parerga and Paralipomena.' Their style is in the highest degree attractive, and their freedom from all formalism and pedantry justifies the encomium bestowed on the writer as 'a philosopher who had seen the world.' They are neither so technical as to be abstruse, nor so long as to be wearisome ; the subjects, moreover, are frequently of general interest. The first volume contains his most lively sallies and some of his most virulent invectives against his sworn foes, the salaried professors of philosophy at the Universities ; it also includes his speculations on apparitions and somnambulism, phenomena in which he beheld the practical confirmation of some of his most original views ; and his maxims, always piquant, often just, on the general conduct of life.

The second volume contains a large number of brief and animated disquisitions on a variety of subjects, including his favourite themes the indestructibility of man's real being by death, on suicide, study, authorship, criticism, and fame.

CHAPTER XI - HIS FAME AND DEATH

LATE in the year 1851 the 'Parerga and Paralipomena' saw the light.

'I am right glad,' Schopenhauer writes, 'to witness the birth of my last child, which completes my mission in this world. I really feel as if a load, that I have borne since my twenty-fourth year, and that has weighed heavily upon me, had been lifted from my shoulder. No one can imagine what that means.'

. . . .

'When we are a little further, I shall be glad to have your candid opinion on the trifles of this *olla podrida* : certainly there will be no want of variety. It is a pasty containing the most various things. In the second volume there are some comic bits, also dialogues. I am much pleased with the printer ; he is attentive and faithful, which please tell him if you have an opportunity.'

The first review gave him keen pleasure. ' It is laudatory throughout, almost enthusiastic, and very well put together. The times of barking and pot-house politics are past. Every one has now to turn to literature.'

This gradual awakening of his fame was a very Indian summer in Schopenhauer's life. He grew more amiable, more accessible ; friends and admirers crowded round him, and though a sneer was hidden in his remark to Gwinner, 'After one has spent a long life in insignificance and disregard, they come at the end with drums and trumpets, and think that is something,' it does not hide the evident satisfaction this tardy recognition afforded.

'My opponents think I am old and shall soon die, and then it will all be over with me ; well, it is already past their power to silence me, and I may live to be ninety.'

The last ten years of his existence were, contrary to custom, the happiest; his 'Parerga' had effected what his more important work had failed to compass. Nothing disturbed the even tenor of his life, and he saw no reason why, with his hale constitution and sensible careful regimen, he should not become a centenarian. The Vedic Upanishad fixes the natural duration of man's life at a hundred; justly so, Schopenhauer thought, as he had remarked that only those who have passed ninety attain Euthanasia, while others who reach the supposed natural age of seventy to eighty die of disease.

Strange to say, it was from England the first signal came that drew attention to Schopenhauer. It was the 'Westminster Review' article, before mentioned, largely read in Germany, and made accessible to all by the German rendering of Dr. Lindner, another of Schopenhauer's new-found disciples. The article gave Schopenhauer the most unfeigned pleasure, and he never tired of speaking its praise.

But best of all,' he writes, 'is the commencement, namely, the picture of my relation to the professors, and the execrableness of these fellows ; above all, the three times repeated—Nothing.'

The fidelity of the translated extracts amazed him : 'The man has rendered not only my style but my mannerisms, my gestures ; it is like a looking-glass—most wonderful!'

'Especially the satirical bits out of the Four-fold Root are admirable.'

'And this in spite of the contempt felt in England for German metaphysics. The extract he has translated is excellently selected, for it exposes the germ and kernel of the nothingness of the University philosophy, and explains why only a lay figure in philosophic garb can live there.'

In the German version, Schopenhauer had first desired the word 'misanthropic' to be suppressed, 'for, in consequence of my recluse life, evil tongues already bandy this word, glad of any handle against me ; 'but, on consideration, he himself re-inserted it in the proof-sheets. Fidelity in translation he held a stern duty.

After the publication of the 'Parerga,' Schopenhauer intended to write no more—he considered he had put the crown to his system ; still he was incessantly occupied with addenda for new editions. He characteristically began to read the German newspapers now that they wrote about him ; he caused even the veriest trifle that contained his name to be sent to him ; he looked through all philosophical works for a mention of himself. Fame warmed his last years with genial rays. The only bane that embittered life was the fear of growing totally deaf, and occasional pangs of horror lest incessant mental labour should throw him into the same dismal state as it had Kant. But he comforted himself with the knowledge of his sounder constitution; the deafness was of course a great trouble.

His little band of disciples grew, and their fanaticism reached a ludicrous point. They came and gazed at him as if he were a stuffed bear : one entreated him to found a trust for the purpose of keeping watch that no syllable of his works should ever be altered; another had his portrait painted and placed in a room like a chapel. He tells his correspondents all these little incidents. 'To-day there came two Russians, two Swedes, and two ladies.' The visits of ladies always perplexed him, though they pleased him. His intense contempt for the sex, to whom he denied all objective interest in art and science, wavered when he saw they could feel it for his works. The University professors still ignored or maligned him, following Don Basilio's maxim in the 'Barbiere di Seville,' 'calumniate;' but he cared less. He was pleased that dilettanti read his writings ; he wanted to be useful to all, not to a clique. ' These rascals,' he said, 'who for thirty-five years have suppressed my birth, now make believe that I am dead ; and if they treat of me at all, treat of me as of an antediluvian fossil. But wait ; I will show you that I am not dead.'

'Their petty stratagem will not help them ; my teaching has already spread too far. An Abyssinian proverb says, "When the Nile is at Cairo, no Dembea (the district where it rises) will be able to stop it." They shall know this. The sympathy of the public increases steadily though slowly, and the boundless enthusiasm of a few, who are becoming many, will guarantee this.'

In 1855 Schopenhauer's portrait was painted in oil, and attracted much notice at the Frankfort Exhibition ; he was also requested to sit for his bust.

'You see the growth of fame follows the laws of conflagration, i.e., it does not proceed in arithmetical but in geometrical or even cubical ratio, and the Nile has reached Cairo! Now the professors may stand on their heads if they like ! *Frustra.* '

The various portraits, photographs, daguerreotypes and busts cannot adequately reproduce a face so full of fire and intellect as Schopenhauer's. The marble head sculptured by Miss E. Ney, now preserved in the Library at Frankfurt, to which it was presented on his death, is considered the best. It was begun in 1859, when Schopenhauer was seventy-one years old. As he would not submit to the mechanical process, it is slightly incorrect in the shape of the face. The sculptress won his high regard ; he lauds her in several letters.

'Perhaps you know the sculptress Ney ; if not, you have lost a great deal. I never thought there could exist so charming a girl. She came from Berlin at the beginning of October to take my bust, and it is so well done and so very like that every one admires it ; and a sculptor has said that none of the artists here could have done it so well.'

To Dr. Frauenstadt he writes :

'Frankfort, March 1, 1856.

'My heartfelt thanks ; old apostle, for your congratulations. To your kind enquiries I can say that I feel little of Saturn's [11] lead : I still run like a greyhound, I am in excellent health, blow my flute almost daily ; in summer I swim in the Main, which I did last on September 19 ; I have no ailments, and my eyes are as good as when I was a student. I only suffer from defective hearing, but this infirmity is hereditary, and troubled me already as a youth. Thirty-three years ago, in consequence of an illness, my right ear became almost deaf, but the left remained sound ; now, since about four years, this begins to fail. It is not noticeable in conversation as long as people are at my left and near me and do not speak particularly low ; but in the theatre it annoys me greatly, even if I sit in the front row of the stalls. I now only go to farces, where there is loud talking ; I shall soon be restricted to the opera. It is a bore!'

Schopenhauer was highly amused at the fair held in Frankfurt in 1857, when a live orang-outang, then a rarity in Europe, was exhibited. He went almost daily to see 'the probable ancestor of our race,' regretting that he had been forced to defer making his personal acquaintance so long. He urged all his friends not to let this opportunity slip by. He was especially struck with its expression, which had not the maliciousness of a monkey's, and by the head, whose frontal bone and *os verticis* were decidedly better formed than those of the lowest human races ; neither did it betray the animal in its gestures. He thought the longing of the Will after cognition was personified in this strange and melancholy beast, and compared his mien to that of the Prophet gazing over into the Promised Land.

'Die Welt als Wille und Vorstellung ' went through a third edition, 'Die Beiden Grrundprobleme der Ethik' a second, for each of which he received an honorarium.

He was actually making money in his old age, he remarked ; the public had not withheld recognition until his death. Thirty years, according to his reckoning, were still before him, in which to taste the sweets of success. He had nothing more to do now but to polish, file, and add ; he could give time to visitors, to perusing the papers, and seeking out all that was written about himself.

'I daresay I do not see half that is written about me. Asher pointed out what was in the "Konstitutionellen" and " Novellen-Zeitung," otherwise I should not have known about it. The latter is a satirical description of my person by Madame B—, because I would not converse with her at table for a whole week. With the notes of these hoped-for conversations she thought to pay her hotel bills.'

Schopenhauer's vigorous health confirmed his expectation of long life ; only once had he shown any sign of weakness, in other respects he continued his manner of living without interruption. But one day in April 1860, as he was hurrying homewards after dinner with his wonted rapid stride, he was overtaken with palpitations and shortness of breath. These uncomfortable symptoms recurred throughout the summer, so that he was forced to shorten his walks and pause for breath, as he would not adopt a slower gait. In August he was attacked by serious illness, but would take no medicines nor obey his physician in essentials. He had an aversion to medicine, and held those fools who hoped to repurchase lost health at an apothecary's. On September 9, Dr. Gwinner found him ill with inflammation of the lungs. 'This is my death,' he said. Nevertheless, he recovered sufficiently in a few days to leave his bed and see friends ; he felt very weak, but began to hope he would pull through, when he was again attacked. Dr. Gwinner was with him on the evening, and gives an account of this his last visit. Schopenhauer was sitting on the sofa, complaining of palpitations, though his voice betrayed no weakness. He had been reading D'Israeli's 'Curiosities of Literature,' and opened at the page treating of authors who have ruined their book-sellers. 'They nearly drove me to that,' he said, jokingly. It did not distress him that his body would soon be eaten by the worms, but he did shiver with horror at the thought of the mangling his spirit would undergo at the hands of the professors of philosophy. He asked what political or literary news there was. The Italian war had interested him greatly from its commencement, though he had felt angry with the 'Times' when it first predicted such a possibility, saying journalists were even more pessimistic in their views than he. He hoped Italy would attain unity, but feared that in that event ancient, individualised Italy, whose divergences in character, spirit, and style had contributed to its might and wondrous culture, would be effaced, to give place to a land levelled to a modern pattern a prophecy which seems in danger of being fulfilled. While the friends conversed it had grown dark; the housekeeper entered with candles, and Gwinner noticed that Schopenhauer's face showed no traces of illness or age. 'It would be miserable if I should have to die now ; I have still important additions to make to the "Parerga."' He remarked that the 'Paralipomena' would have been incorporated with 'Die Welt' had he thought to see its third edition. Then he spoke of the pleasure his celebrity gave him, and showed an anonymous letter received from two Austrian cadets, to which he had vouchsafed a long reply. Still, he added, it would be a pure boon to him if he could attain Nirvana, but he feared death held out no prospect of that. In any case, come what might, he had at least a pure intellectual conscience.

On September 20 Schopenhauer was seized with a violent spasm on rising, so that he fell down and hurt his forehead. Throughout the day, however, he was better, and slept well that night. Next morning he rose as usual, took his cold bath, and breakfasted. His housekeeper had merely let the fresh morning air into his sitting-room, and then absented herself as prescribed. A few moments after the physician entered and found Schopenhauer dead, leaning back in a corner of the sofa. Death had come gently, suddenly, and painlessly. It had been his earnest wish that he might die easily : 'Whoever had been alone all through life must understand that solitary business better than others,' he pleaded.

By his direction no *post-mortem* examination took place, and he was laid in the mortuary chamber longer than customary in Germany. He had a horror of being buried alive. A small strangely mixed assembly congregated round his grave to render him the last honours. A Protestant clergyman performed the service, and pronounced a short funeral oration; then followed Dr. Gwinner with heartfelt words :

His gravesite today.

'The coffin of this rare man, who dwelt in our midst for a generation and yet remained a stranger, evokes unusual reflections. None who stand here are bound to him by the sweet ties of blood ; alone as he lived, he died. And yet in the presence of this dead man something tells us that he found compensation for his loneliness. When we see friend or foe descend, forsaken, into the night of death, our eyes search for a joy that may endure, and every other feeling is stilled in a burning desire to know the sources of life. This ardent yearning after the knowledge of the eternal, which comes to most men only in sight of death, rarely, and evanescent as a dream, was to him the constant companion of a long life. A sincere lover of Truth, who took life seriously, he shunned mere appearances from his very youth, regardless that this might isolate him from all relations human and social. This profound, thoughtful man, in whose breast a warm heart pulsated, ran through a whole lifetime like a child angered at play—solitary, misunderstood, but true to himself. Born and educated in competence, his genius was unhampered by the burdens of this world. He was ever grateful for this great boon ; his one desire was to merit it, and he was ready to renounce all that delights the heart of other men for the sake of his lofty calling. His earthly goal was long veiled to him ; the laurel that now crowns his brow was only bestowed in the evening of life, but firm as a rock was rooted in his soul belief in his mission. During long years of undeserved obscurity he never swerved an inch from his solitary lofty way ; he waxed grey in the hard service of the coy beloved he had chosen, mindful of the saying written in the Book of Esdras : "Great is Truth, and mighty above all things." '

On opening Schopenhauer's will, it was found that his heir was the society founded to support the Prussian soldiers disabled in the revolution of 1848, and the widows and orphans of those who had fallen in their country's service. To Dr. Gwinner, his executor, he left his library ; to Dr. Frauenstadt his philosophical MSS. and the right to publish his works ; and other more trifling legacies. Each of his friends was remembered with a gift : his housekeeper received a munificent sum, and even his poodle was not forgotten ; he left him a yearly income, to be made payable to whomsoever should take charge of him—his housekeeper was to have the first refusal, Dr. Gwinner the second.

Schopenhauer did not wish his biography to be written—he identified his life with his writings ; but these so bear the stamp of his personality, are often so subjective, that while this fact imparts an incontestable charm to his style, it makes an explanation of their source more imperative, and contributes materially towards a harmonious comprehension of the whole. In giving extracts, it was impossible to do justice to his lively and energetic style ; but if our memoir shall induce readers to resort to the fountain-head, and to give this remarkable thinker the fair unbiassed hearing he has hitherto lacked, our labour of love will not be unrewarded.

Notes

See 'Iconoclasm in German Philosophy,' an essay in the 'Westminster Review' for April 1853, understood to be from the pen of Mr. John Oxenford.

Schopenhauer doubtless uses the word in the sense of 'popular; his knowledge of English was pretty exact, as this letter testifies.

Intelligentsia est divina qusedam vis, insita rebus omnibus cum actu cognitionis, qua omnia intelligunt, sentiunt, et quomodoeunque cognoscunt.—Bruno.

Pp. 320 and 440 of the first edition.

Schopenhauer curiously enough makes two misquotations in this little extract from Faust. The original has 'schauen,' not 'sehen ; ' 'dann,' not ' denn.' To disarm criticism, I follow Captain Cuttle's advice, 'when found, make a note of.'

Strange to tell, this, the first cholera visitation, did kill another philosopher ; Hegel, Schopenhauer's favourite butt, fell a victim to it.

She did her best to destroy his felicity, however, by summoning him to her court.

Hamlet, Act I., Scene II. Oehlenschlager, making his first acquaintance with Shakespeare, dashed down the book in disgust at this line, never discovering that what he held to be an indignity to his nationality, was really a compliment.

For an excellent exposition of Kant's ethical system, the reader is referred to Miss F. P. Cobbe's Essay on Intuitive Morals.

Schopenhauer wrote on large sheets of paper folded in half, the one half being left blank for addenda.

This is a reference to the chapter on the ages of man ('Parerga') in which Schopenhauer ascribes the heaviness and dulness of old age to the lead of Saturn, who rules over the sixties.

Made in the USA
Monee, IL
08 November 2023